THE SECRET TO TRANSFORMATIONAL LEADERSHIP

THE SECRET TO TRANSFORMATIONAL LEADERSHIP

DR. QUINTIN SHEPHERD
WITH SARAH WILLIAMSON

http://transformationalleadershipsecret.com

ISBN: 978-0-578-37694-3

"And the end of all our exploring
Will be to arrive where we started
And know the place for the first time."

—T.S. ELIOT in "Little Gidding"

CONTENTS

1 **Introduction: Quintin Shepherd**

7 **Introduction: Sarah Williamson**

13 **How to Use This Book**

17 **Chapter 1: From Competent to Compassionate**

39 Transformational Leadership in Practice: Dr. Linda Stork, Division Head of Pediatric Hematology and Oncology and the Director of the Doernbecher Blood and Cancer Program

47 Chapter 2: From Excuses to Explaining, Trust to Unconditional Faith

61 Transformational Leadership in Practice: Marcus Soutra, President, Eye to Eye

67 Chapter 3: From Accountability to Empowerment, Feedback to Feedforward

77 Transformational Leadership in Practice: Kimberly Smith, Executive Director of the Center for Inclusive Innovation and the League of Innovative Schools, Digital Promise

83 Chapter 4: From Soft Skills to Power Skills

91 Transformational Leadership in Practice: Aseem Giri, Head of Content, Robin

97 Chapter 5: From Work/Life to Life/Work

107 Transformational Leadership in Practice: Bree Langemo, Director of Entrepreneurship and Assistant Professor of Law and Entrepreneurship, Concordia College

115 Chapter 6: From Complicated to Complex

130 Transformational Leadership in Practice: Jeff Patterson, CEO, Gaggle

139 Chapter 7: From Hierarchies to Networks, Management to Leadership

147 Transformational Leadership in Practice: Shaily Baranwal, CEO and Founder, Elevate K-12

155 Chapter 8: From Openness to Radical Transparency to Unprecedented Levels of Accessibility

169 Transformational Leadership in Practice: Bill McCullough, VP Sales, Education Technology

177 Chapter 9: From Engagement to Ownership Commitment to Discipline

183 Tranformational Leadership in Practice: Dave MacLeod, Co-Founder and CEO, ThoughtExchange

195 What's Next?

197 Notes

203 Acknowledgments

INTRODUCTION:

QUINTIN SHEPHERD

"Leading from the middle is the new language of leadership we all must master."

Walk back in time with me, say, one million years, when it was widely believed our ancestors first started using fire. Now imagine you were one of the people who had committed to using fire as part of your daily life, and it was profoundly impactful. You were a "convert" to this new world. If you had tried to explain to your group how fire had changed your life, I suspect your audience would have fallen into one of three groups: 1) Those who wouldn't understand. 2) Those who needed more convincing. 3) Those who immediately grasped the concept and changed.

At this juncture, everything would have begun to shift with respect to how people communicated about cooking, tools, heat, survival, etc. Now let me ask you a question from the present: Have you noticed that the language of leadership has begun to change? Perhaps not in such an impactful way as discovering fire, but there is most certainly a leadership evolution taking place across the country and the globe.

For years, I have noticed some leaders connecting more deeply, not only within their organizations and communities, but also with their employees, stakeholders, and shareholders. I have seen others begin to stumble, falter, or completely disconnect in ways that are unimaginable. We have all seen examples of the "best places to work" and have wondered what is working for them? We have also seen CEOs who have been tossed aside for reasons that seem unfathomable.

For more than a decade, I have been busy leading my organizations while looking for "golden threads" that tie successful leaders together, as well as "landmines" other leaders seem to step on regularly. I became increasingly convinced that the language of leadership needed to evolve in some significant ways.

The daily language we use is powerful. The smallest choices of words matter deeply, not only for us as leaders, but for the people we lead. This is true in both our professional and personal lives. The language we use creates a minute-by-minute daily climate. Your organization is made up of countless individual voices that create and define your climate. After years of leadership, I have come to believe that your organizational culture is approximately five years behind your climate. Whatever is happening today is shaping your future culture.

More importantly, your policies, politics, and structures are approximately five years behind your culture—and thus your climate today will quite literally define your organization in ten years. I cannot emphasize this point enough. Our choice of language creates context and bears with it enormous political and cultural ramifications.

I am endlessly fascinated with the language of leadership and how it profoundly impacts the organizations we lead. Our language is laden with past experiences, past ways of thinking, and past ways of knowing. It is one part responsive to the culture and one part defining of that culture. Like it, or not, the leader casts a long shadow, and our use of language makes, and remakes, culture every day. Equally important is the language others use within our organizations. What are you doing to tap that language, learn that language, and help craft that language?

We live in a highly digitized world, and the leader who is not tapped into this internal network is out of the game before it has even started. The big "aha" from this book is that leadership does not start from the top, or the front, but in the middle. Leading from the middle is the new language of leadership we all must master. I will endeavor to give you tools, tips, and strategies to help make this happen.

I started with myself, becoming my own test subject. As funny as this may sound, it was a bold step for me to walk away from some leadership language and start using this new language. Often my words connected with others—but other times, my words fell flat, and I had to figure out why. Eventually, I discovered my language was having a genuine impact on the culture I was trying to create and maintain. Part of this change meant holding on to this new vocabulary, and part of the change was committing to never using certain phrases or words again.

Frankly, I felt like I had discovered fire.

My new language started to change the way I perceived my organization and, more importantly, my employees. This was big for me. In short order, my language started to change how I approached decision-making, a huge step in my evolution as a leader. These little language decisions started making an even bigger impact within my organization, my community, and my own leadership when others began adopting the same language. It was not long before I began developing frameworks and "big ideas" around this new language.

In some ways, this book is the story of my leadership evolution over the past 15 years, and how I needed to be honest about my own transformation. Almost nothing about this was easy. I have failed often—more times than I can count—and I shall recount many of those failures in the hope that my sharing may impart lessons or, perhaps, a commonality with your own experiences. I will also use my failures as a point of departure if they occurred during moments where I knew that what I was saying wasn't true to my beliefs.

As you read this book, there may be times when the language changes I write about seem like a rather simple step. The hard part will be recognizing just how powerfully the old language has created paradigms and frameworks in your mind that are almost unrecognizable.

When I was taking my coursework to earn my Ph.D., I had a professor who talked about "purposeful strange making," which was his way of forcing himself to become a stranger in his own world. It is impossibly difficult to do this sometimes, as we are largely unaware of the constructs by which we make decisions and view the world. Much of my internal development happened during deep meditation and contemplation of my leadership. I've always said I have an unfair advantage over others because I am a runner. As if it's not bad enough to be a runner, I happen to enjoy long distances, and I have no desire to listen to music or podcasts. My "moving meditation" has amounted to hundreds if not thousands of hours of deep thinking and contemplation. This has always been my leadership "superpower."

While pounding the pavement, I would think about these frameworks that we live by and the many ways in which our language can be an obstacle. In my own leadership transformation, I would arbitrarily say that 5% of my growth happened when I made the language change and the other 95% of my growth was in my own thinking about what the change meant.

As my personal evolution was occurring, I took a bold step and started talking about the language of leadership at conferences, during meetings, in small groups, and just about anywhere else leaders would come together. I began to notice that certain phrases seemed to ring true for leaders regardless of their organization.

As I shared my "fire" with others, some seemed to get it immediately, while others took convincing or needed to practice—and some did not connect with what I was talking about at all. I began thinking about language theory, leadership theory, and organizational theory, and I wanted to come up with something that was not domain specific (to education, banking, industry, or any other field), but would be eminently applicable for all leaders who, like me, felt the world around them was changing and wanted to adopt a new language that fit.

And that's when I met Sarah Williamson. She is, in many ways, a kindred spirit, and it did not take me long to recognize one of her unique geniuses in this world is her ability to craft, hone, and share stories. Through a series of conversations, we landed on the idea to write this book, and she agreed to contribute a variety of perspectives on transformational leadership in practice.

INTRODUCTION:

SARAH WILLIAMSON

"If we can help others think differently and reconsider how we mentor, lead, and partner with one another, ultimately, we will be able to share a new language of leadership that will create a ripple effect of empathy, compassion, kindness, and a sense of purpose for our life's work."

It's rare to discover that you share such a unified sense of purpose as I did when I first met Quintin. We recognized that we each had a message to share about leadership, while seeking a deeper purpose for our life's work. This book is the culmination of our mutual experience and a reckoning of the fragility of life. We both embrace a sense of urgency to not only learn all we can, but to share and apply these learnings with others.

All of us have opportunities to take a left turn, or a right turn, in our careers and our lives, but there are subtle clues along the way guiding those decisions. When we take the time to follow the clues, that is truly when the magic can happen. I like to think this book is the result of that magic.

Throughout my years of working with countless CEOs, school district leaders, and chief marketing officers, I have had opportunities to help these leaders authentically share their messages and tell their stories. From my behind-the-scenes role, I have focused on others, and this perspective has provided eye-opening insights into human nature, leadership, and what really makes a difference with their employees, peers, and fellow leaders.

To provide context for this book, I'd like to begin by telling my own story. It will help you understand what I mean when I talk about embracing the raw, unfiltered aspects of our lives and our careers, all of which has helped guide me to this point on my journey.

I always knew that I wanted to build something of my own: a public relations consulting business where I could call myself an entrepreneur. With that goal in mind, I knew I needed some solid experience first. I spent the first seven years of my career working with a variety of clients across a broad swath of industries before I took the leap and launched my own consulting business.

Around the same time I was hanging out my shingle, I also

discovered that I was pregnant with my first child. The following nine months culminated with the birth of both my son and my business. Things looked bright. I was excited about the future of my company and my growing family. But life has a funny way of surprising you. The next several years turned out to be far different than I could have ever anticipated.

Our son was just a year old when (surprise!), we discovered that we were expecting twins. The fog of having three babies in under two years was more exhausting and mentally draining than I can articulate in this introduction. To keep it brief, I will just say it was a very dark period. Still, I was adamant about keeping my consulting business going during those early years. In fact, it was a nice break from changing diapers and pushing strollers.

We were just emerging from the baby years, our twins turning 2 ½, when I took a deep breath and realized I could do this three-kid thing and keep my business going! We were well on our way to venturing back to normal—but, yet again, life had other plans for us.

During the summer of 2018, as wildfire smoke settled into our Central Oregon community, we noticed that my youngest son, Grant, had developed a cough and was often short of breath. I assumed it was a cold or irritation from the fires—until the day a childcare provider who knew our sons well expressed concern that Grant wouldn't walk up the stairs. I, admittedly, thought he was fine, but I agreed to take him to the doctor anyway.

The doctor was stumped. Through a process of elimination, she decided on a chest x-ray to verify that his lungs were clear. After the x-ray, we waited more than 40 minutes for the doctor to return—and felt the first premonition that something was very, very wrong.

The doctor finally arrived, crying and saying she was so sorry. The x-ray revealed my son had a massive tumor in his chest—a symptom of what they would later diagnose as T-cell acute lymphoblastic lymphoma, a rare form of cancer that is even more rare in children. His tumor was growing so rapidly that it was impacting his airway, and he needed immediate medical attention.

We were life-flighted to Doernbecher Children's Hospital in Portland, where we spent the next week in the intensive care unit, listening to other children code blue throughout the night.

The trauma of waking up one day thinking you have a happy, healthy family, and then fighting for your child's life—and learning the medical terminology for his cancer, the treatment, outcomes, and how to dose his chemo—is indescribable. And throughout the next two years of his treatment, during the months we spent in both our local hospital and the oncology unit of the children's hospital, we learned more than we could have ever imagined about survival, love, kindness, and leadership in the midst of suffering.

You may be wondering why I'm sharing such a personal story in a leadership book, but this experience is exactly why

I was excited to partner with Quintin. Up until our battle with childhood cancer, I never intimately understood how quickly the scales can be tipped in life. Fortunately, our son is doing great now. He very likely will not recur and will live a long, cancer-free life. But throughout our journey, we met many families who did not have the same outcome. Many lost a child or face a lifetime of hospital visits and debilitating illness.

As difficult as our cancer journey was, I knew we most likely would still have our child at the end of it. I continued to work for my clients throughout chemo visits, ambulance transports, and hospital admittances.

I now appreciate every day in a different way. I feel like I have an unlimited capacity to pursue my own dreams. Before, I would regularly say we were "so busy" or life was "crazy," but I have since reframed that thinking. Now I commit to a slower-paced life, a life of deliberate choice and purpose.

I often think of the children we met who lost their lives too early, as well as my son who was a tremendous warrior, and it reaffirms my commitment to living in unabashed pursuit of my goals, without fearing failure, regretting not having enough time, or wondering if I am worthy of my own success.

This book is a compilation of lessons learned from both Quintin's and my lives and from the many leaders we have met along the way. It's our goal to share their messages and their stories. If we can help others think differently and reconsider how we mentor, lead, and partner with one another, ultimately, we will be able to share a new language of leadership that will create a ripple effect of empathy, compassion, kindness, and a sense of purpose for our life's work.

HOW TO USE THIS BOOK

We wrote this book for two audiences. The first is leaders who are embracing the change happening within their organizations and want to evolve and grow their leadership. This book will resonate most with leaders adopting this new language, as they know there are paradigmatic Cultural (Cultural with a capital "C") changes that come with it.

The second audience? Aspiring leaders. We have taught enough university-level leadership courses to know there is a new generation of leaders coming up through the pipeline, and they are begging to use a different language. They know the "old" paradigm of leadership is antiquated and, in some cases, broken. We do not currently have a language or framework of leadership that gives us the opportunity to have genuine and relevant conversations about what it means to lead in this era. We are hopeful our contribution here will advance this conversation.

In short, we've got fire—and it has changed our lives. We want to share this fire with you, so we can learn with you and from you.

In the nine chapters that follow, we will lay out a framework built from small language changes you can make as early as tomorrow and bolder language changes that will take time to introduce and practice to master. You will have to gauge your own tolerance. Some of the bigger changes suggested later in this book might not be right for you or your organization at the present time. Remember, it took me nearly 15 years to fully build an understanding of this new language, and it would be unrealistic to suggest this is something others can adopt over a long weekend.

Chapter 1 is about you, the leader—it starts with you, and it will end with you. The chapters that follow will only "work" and become a genuine part of your leadership if you embrace the changes at a personal level.

Chapters 2 and 3 are what we describe as "Let's stop the blame game." We have all had enough of the rhetoric of blame. People are not afraid of making mistakes, they are afraid of blame. Many organizations have adopted a simple two-step process for ensuring they never make progress tackling their problems. Step one is to make people afraid of problems, and step two is to give them someone to blame when problems inevitably arise.

If we could all agree to stop blaming each other for our problems, the world would change overnight. How do we unring this bell? We don't know, but we do have some suggestions about language we can adopt to advance the conversation. In Chapters 2 and 3, we will connect what we learned in Chapter 1 and expand the framework to the people within our organizations.

Chapters 4, 5, and 6 are language frameworks that will help us better connect our organizations to the people who work in them. This means moving beyond your relationships with individual people and starting to think about the organizations as a whole. And this is where your tolerance for change will start to really be tested.

This is also where we can make big cultural shifts in our organizations and impact deep change. If you could "remap the DNA of your organization," this is where it would happen. Our community and business leaders bemoan the fact that people just don't get involved anymore, or people don't care about our future—and although this might be true, we will look at how we can start to turn this conversation in a more productive direction.

In these first six chapters, we talk in generalities about organizations and about the people who work within them. The last three chapters on the languages of leadership jump into the void, so to speak. This feels like a new frontier—and when it's done right, it can have the power of a fire-powered freight train.

We have experienced things as a leader that we couldn't begin to describe 10 years ago ... we simply didn't have the language. This will impact how you as a leader work with your board and employees, with constituents if you're in politics, or with shareholders if you're in business. It will potentially redefine your role as a leader.

So let's ease our way toward the void together.

CHAPTER 1

FROM COMPETENT TO COMPASSIONATE

Leadership. We have heard this term for millennia, and we believe we have a good idea of what it means. We might describe it as someone who is directing others while casting a vision or unifying a group to achieve a common goal. However, one of the most automatic assumptions we make is that leadership requires influence and power.

This definition is affirmed by Merriam-Webster, which states that leadership is "the office or position of a leader [who] recently assumed the leadership of the company; the act or an instance of leadership; leadership molds individuals into a team." Even the example that Merriam-Webster references when using leadership in a sentence that seems to affirm the philosophy that "what this country needs is the exercise of strong leadership!"

Based on this definition and our life experiences, it seems evident that to be a leader we need to be not only good—and effective—at what we do, but we must embody a sense of strength and power.

Spoiler alert: We do not agree with that. Nor do we agree that the future of leadership can be so narrowly defined. Our goal throughout this chapter (and the rest of the book) is to raise questions on how to understand what someone in a leadership role can do. We want to establish fresh parameters around our long-held beliefs and the key elements of leadership that are missing within this historical definition.

When we have leadership roles, we are very often responsible for influencing outcomes, numbers, bottom lines, and budgets; for navigating the political landscape; and for meeting (or exceeding) the expectations of our boards of directors, school boards, venture capitalists, and other financial stakeholders. Pulling away from these mounting pressures can feel impossible.

It's not. There is another path to high achievement, success, and beating insurmountable odds without following the "traditional" course. It's a path that will certainly require more of you as a person, as a human being, and as a guide. Be forewarned: When we embrace humanity, authenticity, and transformation, the results are life changing.

We believe if you apply this work within your teams and bring these ideas forth within your organizations, businesses, government institutions, and schools, several things will happen. Yes, you will undoubtedly see higher productivity from your staff and teammates. You will also have total visibility into what your community expects of you and what you expect of them. Most importantly, however, you will transform what you thought was possible. Together, you will be able to achieve more than you ever dreamt possible.

When the idea for this book began to germinate, we reached out to our LinkedIn community and asked, "Were there times in your leadership career when you felt being a competent leader got in the way of being a compassionate leader?"

One of the many responses we received, the most poignant was simply two words: "Every day." Our community overwhelmingly affirmed that this was a topic others would be interested in. Countless people encouraged us to keep writing and talking about this.

Competent Leadership Gets the Job Done, But ...

Give yourself a moment to think about competent leadership. Think of an example or two of competent leaders you know so we can map this word and this space together. These people you are thinking of need to be a little better than average. They do not necessarily have to be great, but they are competent. These leaders can get the job done more often than not, and you don't have to "manage" them. I have become increasingly convinced that if someone must be closely managed after the initial onboarding period, they are not the right fit. This is true for every position and in every level of our organizations.

Once you have competent leaders in mind, think about what makes them competent. They know their job and the skill sets required for success. They know how to manage their time and responsibilities. They can put out fires within the organization with relative ease. They can cover a wide array of issues in any number of areas.

People become competent through education and experience. I worked to become competent when I started as a leader. So did you, if you're being honest. I needed to become competent in human resources, finance, governance, and other aspects of my duties. My education and my training were built around this notion of competence. Learn stuff, apply stuff, repeat as necessary. Like you, I discovered my aptitude in some areas of my competencies was greater than in others. Eventually, as I became more competent, there were parts of my job that I started to think of myself as good at. Others may have said I was good as well. My evaluations and feedback were designed around my competence.

Perhaps the most important example from my own leadership comes from negotiations. I have negotiated personnel contracts, union contracts, service contracts, performance contracts, and more. Early in my career, contract negotiations were all about competence. “Good” contracts were win/lose propositions. My ability to negotiate a good contract meant it was either good for me directly or good for my organization.

I fell into this mindset rather easily, considering my first few union contract negotiations were total failures! In the world of win/lose, I lost badly. Usually, my negotiations ended up with raised voices. They were highly tense or emotional, and I generally walked away from those experiences feeling horrible. While the contracts themselves were a “loss” for me, even worse was the feeling I had when they were concluded.

I began to study everything I could get my hands on, attending conferences, reading every book available on negotiations ... including several texts on game theory. In short order, I became good, and eventually better than good. I gained some notoriety as a successful negotiator in my circles and was asked to help consult with others on contract negotiations. I went from a “loser” to a “winner”—and regardless of the outcome, I still walked away from the table feeling like everyone lost.

Somehow, being competent didn’t fulfill my promise as a leader. Being competent actually worked against my leadership beliefs. But I couldn’t articulate that at the time. I was good, and I was unfulfilled. Not a great combination.

This antiquated leadership paradigm, based on the notion of competence, gets hung up before it even gets started. If I am stuck in a paradigm of competence, it means I am also stuck on a continuum of bad and good. If I am incompetent at a certain task, I am bad at that task and will receive a bad rating. If I am really good at a task, I might be great. Either way, when I frame the work I am doing as a leader around the language of competence, I have locked myself into a paradigm of good and/or bad.

> *"It is not the critic who counts: not the man who points out how the strong man stumbles or where the doer of deeds could have done them better. The credit belongs to the man who is actually in the arena, whose face is marred by dust and sweat and blood, who strives valiantly; who errs and comes short again and again, because there is no effort without error and shortcoming, but who knows the great enthusiasms, the great devotions, who spends himself in a worthy cause; who, at the best, knows, in the end, the triumph of high achievement, and who, at the worst, if he fails, at least he fails while daring greatly, so that his place shall never be with those cold and timid souls who neither know victory nor defeat."*
>
> —THEODORE ROOSEVELT

This quote is presented often in the context of big, bold leadership. Quotes like this—and countless others—create a language of leadership. The critics sit on the sidelines while the leader is bloodied in the arena.

With all due respect to President Roosevelt, this is the antiquated paradigm, and it wonderfully articulates a leadership paradigm that no longer exists. We teach upcoming leaders that they should "keep their friends close and their enemies closer"—and this idea has some merit, but it also isn't the answer.

The new language of leadership allows us to open the door to the critic to be a part of the effort. The new language of leadership finds no leader alone in "the great devotions, who spends himself." The new language of leadership embraces the digital world we live in and recognizes the "lone wolf" leader as truly being a thing of the past.

Leadership from the middle asks us to bring everyone in just a little closer to make their voices heard. Step into the conversation, not above it. I picture the "old guard" leadership reading this and shaking their heads. *Perhaps, it sounds good on paper, but can it really be done? How does one capture the voice of all?*

I am not the first to recognize this evolving nature of leadership. In *Leadership on the Line: Staying Alive Through the Dangers of Leading*, Ronald Heifetz and Marty Linsky write, "To lead people, we suggest you build structures of relationships to work the tough issues ... to let people do the work that only they can do" (p. 122). This book, and countless others, point in an opposite direction of individual leadership competence, but still they are scant on two important areas. First, they fail to provide language for this different type of leadership. Second, there are very few real-world examples of how to put this type of leadership to work.

Let me give a real-world example from my own experience. When I first moved to Victoria, Texas, I knew it as a place that had recently been devastated by Hurricane Harvey. I didn't live there through the hurricane but came shortly thereafter. As a school district, we knew our fund balances had been depleted as we were starting the initial phases of hurricane remediation. Federal emergency relief and insurance funds hadn't yet started flowing. We had a one-time opportunity to raise taxes through a hurricane relief provision in the Texas Tax Code. So, within my first 30 days on the job, I had to introduce the idea of a tax increase to the community.

We could've simply enacted the tax without public input as an emergency action, but this is not my style of leadership. Raising taxes is generally a bad thing (note the language of competence) even if it does a good thing (financial solvency). Bad and good are not my language. I needed the community to understand my suffering. We endeavored to be "radically transparent" and open as many doors as possible to our community. We went through town hall forums, social media outlets, local news—and we sent the message that we welcomed all questions and concerns from our community. We utilized a digital tool to ensure it wasn't just the loudest voices that were heard, but the best thoughts. We crowd-sourced our community around this tax increase.

When it came time for our decision, 30 days later, not a single person claimed they did not have the opportunity to be heard. All told, there were thousands of points of interaction (mostly digitally). That's how we established a climate of leading from within.

Competent leadership is based on notions of "good" and "bad," and, as a result, it is highly polarizing. In my example above, raising taxes is good if you want to ensure financial stability for the school district and bad if you are a homeowner without a vested interest in education. The decision resulting from competent leadership is to create winners and losers. Hence the polarization.

On a more theoretical level, if you have ever sat through a leadership class, you know it takes no time at all before somebody brings forward some horrific leader from our past and asks something like, "How do we define 'leadership' when we know there are good leaders and bad leaders?" In short order, the class has devolved into trying to figure out what makes a leader good or bad. Pretty soon, everyone shrugs their shoulders, and the group tries to come up with some working definition that seems to fit all leadership. The result is either so vague or so endlessly mind-numbing that we stumble through the conversation just to get it over with.

I'm going to ask you to back away from competency-based leadership and completely reframe what a leader does.

Leadership is a function, which is to say, it answers this

question: What does leadership do? Once you answer this question for yourself, you are nearly ready to walk away from competency-based leadership language. It took me close to ten years in leadership positions across multiple states to figure out my answer to that question.

My answer is not your answer. So, I will ask you again: What does *your* leadership do? I suspect, if you are honest, somewhere deep down you might not know the answer. If so, please take a moment to celebrate! While I don't have all the answers, I do think I have a few good questions, and this question is at the heart of everything that follows.

Even if you have a leadership definition that connects with you already, I hope you will allow me to share my thoughts with you. After years of reading countless books on the subject, the definition that has always made the most sense to me is: "Leadership is an influence relationship among leaders and followers who intend real changes that reflect their mutual purposes" (Rost, p. 102).

A slightly more expanded view on leadership is as follows.

1. The relationship is based on influence:

a. The influence relationship is multi-directional.

b. The influence behaviors are non-coercive.

2. Leaders and followers are the people in this relationship:

a. The followers are active.

b. There must be more than one follower, and there is typically more than one leader in the relationship.
c. The relationship is inherently unequal because the influence patterns are unequal.

3. **Leaders and followers intend real changes:**
    a. "Intend" means that the leaders and followers purposefully desire certain changes.
    b. "Real" means that the changes the leaders and followers intend must be substantive and transforming.
    c. Leaders and followers do not have to produce changes in order for leadership to occur. They intend changes in the present; changes take place in the future if they take place at all.
    d. Leaders and followers intend several changes at once.

4. **Leaders and followers develop mutual purposes:**
    a. The mutuality of these purposes is forged in the non-coercive influence relationship.
    b. Leaders and followers develop purposes, not goals.
    c. The intended changes reflect, not realize, their purposes.
    d. The mutual purposes become common purposes.

Let me be clear on what this book is not. This is not a book that sets out to completely redefine leadership. The working definition above meets my standard for a definition of leadership. Instead, this book is focused on the question *What does leadership do?* and, more specifically, what the language of leaders does as a function of their leadership. Leaders can be polarizing, divisive, aggressive, subservient, humble, bold, demeaning, inspiring, etc. The list is endless. Leaders choose their language (sometimes carefully)—and this language has far-reaching implications.

The leadership language we will be talking about throughout this book is one that embraces the digital world we live in, the generational differences we all face in the workforce, the need to accomplish organizational goals, and the need to help bring people together around ideas. This is language that will inspire and empower at the same time. It will unite people around difficult issues, as opposed to dividing them. This is language that will focus equally (or person even more) on great questions over satisfactory answers. It is language that embraces the unknown and wrestles it into the manageable.

As stated previously, a good/bad competence leadership frame is highly polarizing. As you read the definition above, true leadership would be the exact opposite, a phrase I have come to call "constructive di-polarization." Constructive di-polarization is bringing people together around purposes and relationships and not dividing people based on ideas.

Often, in the chapters that follow, we will suggest you pause or stop reading and take a moment to really think deeply. It is easy to read endlessly and never connect with what you are reading, but we are genuinely interested in your growth—and the only way for new knowledge to have any meaning for you is for you to take time and connect this new knowledge with old knowledge. That reflection can only be done through deep metacognition (thinking about your thinking).

My personal orientation to learning new things is called epistemological relativism. Basically, I think of your brain as covered in Velcro. You know a bunch of stuff, and the only way to learn new stuff is to connect the new stuff to the old stuff.

Reflections Toward a New Paradigm

I have just put a few big ideas in front of you, related to how you define leadership and how you understand the purpose of your leadership. Stop and think about this question: *What does your leadership do right now? What is it meant to be doing?*

Hopefully you were able to think of your organization as well as some real and intentional goals—and how you are working with the people in your organization to achieve these goals. Let's tug on this notion of competence and relate it to what you were thinking about. You can instantly start connecting dots about where you are successful and where you aren't—and almost immediately, things fall into the "good" or "bad" continuum.

It is amazing how fast that paradigm in our head takes shape almost without conscious thought. It is going to take effort to move away from it. That's the "old stuff" in our brain, and it has created a worldview for us. We need to do more than disrupt our thinking. We need to completely dislodge our thinking by asking tough questions.

When you think of the goals of your organization or your personal goals, how do you define success? Does your mind immediately fall into a competence-based framework of success?

Isn't this fascinating?

In *Primal Leadership*, we learn that "leaders cannot lead with resonance if their team's norms hold them captive. And they cannot change the team's norms unless they are willing to take on the leader's primal task: working with people's emotions and with the team's emotional reality" (Goleman, Boyatzis, & McKee, p. 189).

In this passage, we recognize the signature of a new call for leadership but without a language change or practical steps to be taken. Further, "to create the vision of a company, emotionally intelligent leaders need to move beyond a solo scrutiny of an organization's vision to drawing on the collective wisdom of follows. Side-by-side, with the rest of the organization, leaders co-create the vision that will serve to rally and energize the group as a whole." This sounds wonderful, but note the lack of any practical advice about how to actually make that happen.

In the introduction, I posited that our climate begets our

culture, and our culture becomes our politics and policies. This process realistically unfolds in about a decade. Part of the reason for scant practical advice is that very few leaders or organizations have created policies that allow for this type of culture to thrive. This makes those rare examples where it does exist non-duplicative.

The practical advice for you is to start changing the language by connecting more deeply with your current climate. Immerse yourself in crowd-sourcing decisions (not all decisions; you will read much more on the nuances of this in Chapter 7) and optimizing digital strategies to create shared and equitable spaces for everyone to have their voices heard.

In the chapters that follow, I want to honor the leaders who have come before us. I am compelled to state that competence leadership is not a bad thing. Competence leadership was a critical, necessary, and essential first step for us to take in defining leadership, going back to the late 1700s, according to well-documented histories. However, Bernard Bass, who developed the transformational leadership theory, tells us that scientific research on leadership did not begin until the 20th century.

Our leadership ancestors needed to create some language that would make sense for their culture and their society. For previous generations, conversations about competence were exactly the right conversations. They inhabited a different culture in a different time. Our leadership ancestors were not wrong. They did not live in the digital era we do, where our CEOs can be seen every day on TV, YouTube, Facebook, Instagram, or every other social media outlet.

Most employees would not have had access to executive-level leadership, where competence could take a front seat. Further, previous generations had a different orientation to work, organizations, and leadership. Current and forthcoming generations are routinely described as having less respect for established leadership. I think nothing could be further from the truth. They covet leadership that represents the collective voice. It is with both honor and respect that I thank our former leaders for mapping the territory for us. It is with that same respect that I am now calling on us to reconceptualize the paradigm, given that the times have changed.

Introducing Compassion-Based Leadership

If we walk away from competence-based leadership as a value judgement (good or bad) and introduce compassion-based leadership, we need to redefine this space. Let's use the same cognitive tool we used to start the chapter. Think of someone you would describe as a compassionate leader. This does not necessarily mean someone who is nice, loving, or soft. If we break the word "compassion" down, we know the Latin "com" is a prefix meaning "with," "together," "in association," and (with intensive force) "completely." Looking at the word "passion," we find that it means "suffering." I hope this gives you pause ... it should. Compassion is to be with others completely in their suffering—and I hope you are wondering how in the world this connects to leadership.

The compassionate language asks us as leaders to immerse ourselves fully. While competent language asks us to partition, break apart, and objectify, compassionate language instead invites us to break down walls, to immerse ourselves fully, to think in holistic terms, to feel, to care, and to embrace.

I want for you to hold onto this point: to suffer is to care.

It's a big shift from competence to compassion. Competence does not require you to care. How many leaders can we point to who might be effective in their jobs, but deep down we know they don't care? We see it whenever a CEO has been effective but somehow just didn't connect with either employees or stakeholders. We are convinced it is why some seemingly qualified politicians lose elections. They might be experts in aspects of governance and fully competent in every way, but voters detect their lack of compassion.

Competence becomes a landmine for leaders. This should cause all leaders who are engaged in mentoring or teaching future leaders some alarm, since nearly all our training and education programs are built around competence. We have been brought up in a paradigm that will potentially cause our undoing. We are training future leaders to create their own minefields. Does anybody else feel this is wrong? This explains why many students in leadership classes intuitively know that what they are learning isn't "real life" or is all theory with no practicality.

The longer our brains tug at this thought, the more we are convinced we all need to reset the language we are using around leadership development programs if we are going to make any forward progress.

Further, if we can look to other leaders and see how and why compassion is a much better framework for having conversations about the type of leadership we want in them, we need to look in the mirror as well and accept the reality that it is a better language for us too.

My wise friend, business leader Dave MacLeod, once reminded me, "Before we can be compassionate with others, we first must be compassionate with ourselves." We need to embrace our own suffering.

I'd like to pause here and embrace the fact that both Sarah and I suffered to even start this writing project. We don't consider ourselves experts, and we don't pretend to have all the answers. We do have some life leadership experiences and have learned a great deal through conversations with other leaders, as well as endless reading on the subject. We suffered with how we can present information to push your thinking while being genuine about the fact that we've made countless mistakes along the way and will probably make more in the future. Being compassionate with ourselves allows us to find authenticity in our leadership.

To that end, I want to revisit my own experience with negotiations. I have come to realize compassionate leadership can be prominently displayed in the context of contract negotiations. Within my personal negotiations, there has been a willingness to share my needs but also to genuinely explore the needs of others. For example, contract negotiation involves embracing union members' needs as well as one's own, and this understanding has allowed me to negotiate many agreements that I feel are truly win/win.

As I embraced compassionate leadership, not only did I negotiate successful contracts, but I was able to walk away from more negotiations with a sense of deep partnership toward everyone involved. It is not that the relationships were more important than the outcome. Rather, the relationships *drove* the outcome.

Early in the chapter, we proposed that leadership is a function, and we shared Rost's definition that it is an "influence relationship among leaders and followers who intend real changes that reflect their mutual purposes." This all still holds true, and we want you to realize that competence in the leadership framework caused you to think in a very specific way.

We have introduced you to compassionate leadership. This, hopefully, causes a hiccup in your thinking because compassionate leadership means you will judge the very act of leadership and its function differently. The competence-based language of leadership is like a suit that doesn't quite fit right anymore. It works and gets the job done, but you know it is not as good as it could be.

Compassion-based language allows you to say things like, "I threw myself fully into this project because it mattered to our organization and here is what we learned." We can begin to walk away from "good" or "bad" and have a genuine and serious conversation about transformative leadership, complex change, and culture.

So many leadership evaluations seem to want to tackle the big and hard topics, but competence language gets in the way of having the conversations that matter. Compassion gives us the chance to think differently about how we might evaluate our efforts.

Compassion-Based Learning as a Sign of Promise

If you want to find signs of progress in this area, we will offer up the field of education. Two specific areas of education are undergoing massive transformations. First, we see examples of "schools that work." This is a very broad definition of any school that has re-designed the student learning experience around the student. Second, we see a monumental shift in student, parent, and teacher perceptions of competency-based assessment.

There are schools around the country embracing compassion over competence. You will find it wherever students are given the opportunity to immerse themselves fully in their education. We know technology-based education is not for every student, but it definitely works for some. When they are given the autonomy to explore and design their curriculum, students almost always perform better on competency-based assessments. Similarly, when students are given an opportunity to learn in project-based learning environments (by choice, not by chance or requirement), they thrive.

Students who are allowed to throw themselves into their learning with passion demonstrate both higher and deeper learning. There are a growing number of books on this topic, and some of the pioneering work in collecting these success stories can be found in venture capitalist, entrepreneur, and author Ted Dintersmith's education initiative *What School Could Be*.

We receive proof that competence frameworks do not fit the paradigm of compassion frameworks when we see students who are wildly excited about their learning through a unit or semester only to be deflated by the need to assess competence. The two frameworks do not work together because one is based on teaching, measuring, and sorting, and the other seeks to be relevant as it bolsters students' acquisition and application of knowledge. To pretend we can use compassion-based learning in a competence-based framework is foolish at best and downright harmful at worst. This is why so many teachers, parents, and students are starting to speak up against competence-based language. We are collectively beginning to realize a new language is needed. Compassionate school leadership, compassionate teaching, and compassionate learning fit with our current needs ... we just need to start using our language.

To illustrate how this national education movement intersects with the workplace, I will ask you what kind of leaders you hire? How do you rate them? How do you evaluate them? I have used so many tools and instruments over my career, I have lost count. Most are adequate, good, or even great ... at measuring competence. None answer the one question that really matters to me as CEO: "Would I want to work for this person?"

Years ago, I told myself I would not hire nor keep someone on my leadership team who wasn't someone I would want to work for. When I recognize that someone is a compassionate leader, the answer is always a resounding yes, I would want to work for them. I know I would be challenged, inspired, cared for, held responsible, supported, etc.

We will write more about evaluations in the next chapter, because this permeates every aspect of leadership, from education and mentoring to assessments and dismissal. Our current reality is that competence leadership has mapped the terrain, defined the context, and structured the conversation around leadership, whether we like it or not. Compassionate leadership doesn't fit in this antiquated model, and there are some who are quick to discard it because of that.

If you are thinking compassionate leadership just isn't for

you, we suggest you save a lot of time and give this book to someone else. Don't bother reading anymore. Everything that follows is built upon this premise.

Others of us see the fire. We are out actively hiring people we would work for because we are trying to seek out compassionate leaders. We may not have great frameworks to teach it (yet). We may not have figured out how to evaluate it (yet). Regardless, we are committed to this new paradigm because we know this is the language of leadership that matters in our organization.

Our humble suggestion is we all start calling it what it is and start building the education and evaluation frameworks allowing us all to make forward progress in developing the compassionate leadership we so desperately need.

TRANSFORMATIONAL LEADERSHIP IN PRACTICE

DR. LINDA STORK

Division Head of Pediatric Hematology and Oncology and the Director of the Doernbecher Blood and Cancer Program

Although she now holds a leadership role at the Doernbecher Blood and Cancer Program in Portland, Oregon, Linda Stork initially questioned if she was cut out for the medical profession. When she started in pediatric hematology/oncology, more than forty percent of her patients died. "If I had had my son before I chose my sub-specialty, I wouldn't have been able to do this job—but I was already so invested that I stuck with it," she said.

She generously shared her lessons learned from more than forty years of serving as a pediatric oncologist and what her patients—both dead and alive—have taught her about life, leadership, and compassion.

Expressing Compassion

"When I arrived at Doernbecher from my previous role as a physician in Denver," Linda said, "the culture was very unusual. The general philosophy was not to discuss anything emotional. I remember very clearly, at one of our very first conferences with nurse practitioners, we were discussing an adolescent patient who was terminal and dying. There was a discussion about what to do, and I naively said, 'Well, what are his thoughts about death?' I had used the word death, and people looked at me like, 'What kind of a crazy question is that?'

"I was pulled aside later by a very astute nurse practitioner who shared with me that this was the first time the word death had ever been used in a conference room that she could remember. That amazed me, because we are talking about pediatric oncology, where it's life and death all the time—but somehow, this was stuff you just weren't supposed to talk about.

"I didn't believe those physicians were not compassionate," Linda reflected. "They were very compassionate, but they weren't allowed to culturally show it. And I don't know where that comes from. It was different from my previous experience. I remember walking from the parking lot to my office not long after that day, when I said to myself, 'There are a lot of people who are really bright around here, and a lot of people who are brighter than I am. What can I bring to this program that is unique?' My answer was, undoubtedly, compassion."

Linda still doesn't know if you can teach a person to feel compassion, but she does believe you can teach those who possess it how to express it. From that day forward, her goal was to help other physicians, many of whom were male, by granting them permission to express their emotions and not to be afraid of them.

Embrace Humanism

"Many years ago," Linda said, "a patient came to the emergency room with a very large mediastinal mass, was nearly dead, and needed urgent attention. [From Sarah: My son also had a mediastinal mass, so I clearly understand how life-threatening this can be and feel.] This was back when the physicians took patient blood pressure with a listening cuff, and I could tell by the blood pressure sounds that her heart was constricted.

"I immediately called cardiology and told them they had to stick a needle in the mass, and they had no time to waste. I just knew it. Well, it was pretty stressful. As this was happening, I talked to the patient's mother, and, of course, I was emotional, because it was a very stressful situation. Fortunately, the patient did survive. About two weeks later, the social workers said to me, 'I want to tell you something that this mother said. She said that when you spoke with her, you had tears in your eyes, and when she saw your tears, she knew she could trust you with anything.'"

Linda felt that, once again, this gave her permission to be human. "Clearly physicians are tasked with being as composed as possible—especially during a stressful situation. There are, however, times that require of us deep human emotions, and that was one of the most important lessons for me as a doctor, and as a human being, to hear from that parent. At the time, I recalled feeling bad that I couldn't compose myself. But hearing that from the social worker about this mother validated that it was okay. It made me realize being human with our patients, and demonstrating empathy and compassion, is okay."

Be Honest—Especially When It's Hardest

"Early in my career," said Linda, "I recall many people talking about the book *Sadako and the Thousand Paper Cranes*, a children's historical novel written by Canadian American author Eleanor Coerr. The book is about a girl who developed leukemia after the bombing of Hiroshima, and she was in the hospital. Throughout the book, I could feel the fear that this young child was experiencing because people weren't talking to her. Instead, she was told that if she could make 1,000 origami cranes, she would live.

"And the reason I hate this book so much," Linda continued, "is because everyone is lying to her, and it's not fair. She was six or seven years old, and you can tell that there's something that isn't being said. And I think most of us working in pediatric oncology believe that a child at a very young age gets it. Clearly you don't have to tell a three-year-old that your chance of cure is xx percent. But you need to listen to them and let them express themselves however they need to do that. It's important that we listen to a patient with both our eyes and our ears."

Take Care of Yourself

A lot of the emotional trauma from the experience of childhood cancer isn't just the life or death, it's the side effects. It's the chemotherapy, the spinal taps, the nausea, the transfusions, the amount of time the child is in the clinic and in the hospital instead of in school. All of that impacts the physicians as well.

Linda highly encourages her team to take vacations. She knows that if they get away—truly get away—they will be better physicians, more able to recover and to manage their own emotional needs and the needs of their patients.

"Years ago," said Linda, "I had been practicing for almost 20 years, and a mother of a patient of mine decided to interview me for something. I don't remember what it was. I was at a point where I cried as I talked through that entire interview. I had no reserve. And I said to her, 'I feel as though I have chronic PTSD.' That wasn't even really a concept then except after war. But I told her that I just didn't get the time to breathe and feel one thing before I go to another. Sometimes in the clinic I might see three patients: One I would have to tell there's no chance of cure. The second one, I might give them a new diagnosis. The third one, I might give them their chemo, and I'd be happy to see they're doing well. There was never any time to debrief, which is why taking a break is so important for all of us."

Do What Lights You Up

Linda strongly believes "that women entering medicine have driven it to be so much more humanistic than it used to be. There's many more females—nurses and physicians—leading the care of this hospital than men now. And so, innately, I think there's much more comfort in expressing emotion.

"I think we need to be able to develop comfort combining compassion with the science of medicine—the intellectual art, but also the humanistic art," she reflected. "Things are continuing to shift in this direction, and medical schools are now seeking applicants with aspects of humanism.

"I used to say, 'In my previous life, what did I do so wrong that I'm redeeming myself with this profession?' I mean, I'm teasing, but not completely. My saying that was primarily driven by what we experienced back then when so many more kids died. And when systems just didn't help. Our systems are so much better now. Our nurses are so much more independent. Our administrators get it.

"If I hadn't gone into pediatric oncology, I would have gone into international medicine and worked in poverty or something like that—some other form of suffering. It's just in me," she said. "The bottom line is, I'm just more alive doing this work, and I will do it tomorrow, and the next day, and the day after that."

CHAPTER 2

FROM EXCUSES TO EXPLAINING, TRUST TO UNCONDITIONAL FAITH

Excuses, excuses, excuses ... sometimes it can feel like an endless line of excuses. In our personal lives, we hear children giving excuses to their parents and teachers. In our careers, we have heard countless excuses from countless employees. We have all delivered our own share of excuses. Excuses fall flat, however. An excuse feels like a failure—because it is.

To fail at something is to apply a value judgement of good and bad—and therein lies the problem. No matter the type of leader you set out to be, I do not think you set out to get excuses from your employees. Human resources consultant Patty McCord, author of *Powerful: Building a Culture of Freedom and Responsibility* and formerly the chief talent officer at Netflix, explains it well when she says, "Here is my radical proposition: A business leader's job is to create great teams that do amazing work on time. That's it" (p. xvii).

In your evolution as a compassionate leader, once you realize you are part of the problem, you will quickly realize you need to be part of the solution.

In Chapter 1, we touched on the notion of competence, which, as a mental construct, forces us into a judgement paradigm of "good" or "bad." Bad can lead to failure, which necessitates an excuse.

In this chapter and the next, we will explore the ramifications of this construct and introduce some language and thinking paradigms that will allow us to move in a different direction.

As author Daniel Pink (2011) notes about the connection between individual and organizational purpose, "Too many organizations—not just companies, but governments and nonprofits as well—still operate from assumptions about human potential and individual performance that are outdated, unexamined, and rooted more in folklore than in science" (p. 9). With competence and judgement frameworks in place, the logical language in response is to give an excuse.

When a child demonstrates a lack of competence at taking out the trash, for example, we cannot be surprised when they respond in the language of excuse. We all love the stories about a child who stops making excuses through some magical process and begins to take pride in their work, but how does that actually happen?

One of the first steps in the evolution toward compassionate leadership is moving away from excuse-based language. We will make this point over and over again throughout this book: The language we use is the climate we create now, and that will become our culture and policies five and ten years from now.

Changing your language today is critical for our future.

It might be easy to think about children's excuses as cute or even comical, but what about when employees make excuses? Often, this isn't so funny. The general storyline goes something like this: A manager calls the employee into the office and tells them what they did (or did not do). The employee then responds with an excuse ("I wasn't trained," "I didn't know," etc.).

Sometimes the process is quick, and sometimes it takes months. Sometimes the employee grows from the experience, but often the employee and manager walk away with the same thought. *That won't happen again.* The employee may want to avoid getting caught, or they may be compliant in the future, but they almost never feel heard or appreciated.

Yes, appreciated. How could an employee ever feel appreciated in this situation?

Further, the manager thinks this will not happen again because they have spoken with the employee, shown them the error of their ways, corrected the behavior, and gotten back to work.

Does the manager feel fulfilled? Almost certainly not.

If the manager's job is competence-based at remediating behavior, that is the focus. The manager is judged "good" for correcting the behavior. A manager in competence mode is both creating and perpetuating the problem. The fault in this scenario largely rests with the manager who perpetuates competence-based paradigms.

This is what we mean by climate creating culture and policy. We are quite literally living our commitment to competence. We cannot be surprised the employee has the same surface-level response, because we have written it into policy. As Patty McCord writes, "Are we limited by the team we have not being the team we should have?" (p. 76).

Here's a brief thought experiment. Take a moment and think of your human resources department and its processes. How many competence-based policies and practices can you list and describe?

Bernard Bass, whose work we referenced in Chapter 1, felt that many leaders make the critical mistake of placing too much emphasis on either the task to be done or the relationship with others. Bass described leaders as either task-focused or follower-focused. These provided great bookends to the conversation about competence leadership. Bass' work stands as a seminal piece of writing in leadership theory, and it has been referenced often over the past 40 years. The prominence of his work has become an institutionalized paradigm of thinking ... but it may not serve our leadership purpose today.

Logically, Bass encouraged a balanced emphasis. We want to pull on this concept with you. Bass identified a leadership model still rooted fully in competence at either end of the spectrum. On one end of the spectrum is "task focus." On the other end is "follower focused."

Compassionate leadership, on the other hand, is neither task nor follower-focused but exists at a deeper level. It embraces the task focus *and* the follower focus fully and creates a space where both can coexist peacefully. True compassionate leadership is a zero-sum game and can create a win-win scenario.

A compassionate leader who wants to have compassionate employees—those who are fully immersed, fully present, and emotionally attached—will actively resist an excuse conversation. It is antithetical to their belief system. Likewise, a compassionate parent who is raising compassionate children will tactfully and purposely avoid excuse-based conversations.

Total transparency here: This was insanely hard when we first dedicated ourselves to this new language of leadership. When we found ourselves heading down the excuse hole, we had to retrain and unlearn our default response while backing away from the conversation so we could start over at a different time. Think of it as a time out on the field, a false start moment, when the team has to reset five yards and try again.

In your leadership journey, your children, your spouse, and your closest friends will be your test subjects, and once you start making progress (with yourself, not with them), you will begin to apply this to your leadership. Be prepared to fail. This work is hard, and you will have many false starts. Regardless of where you are on your leadership journey, you have been inculcated in a competence and excuse culture. As you make this shift, you will notice when the excuse presents itself. At that moment, take a break and reframe. Your future success lies in your ability to notice it first and ultimately forestall it from happening altogether. Eventually, your climate will become your culture.

You will become a test subject too. For example, how often do you fail at your own goals? And what happens when you do? Do you make an excuse?

Why is it that our minds immediately fall into excuse-based language? Many times, we fail because our competence language says something like, "I will lose 15 pounds in the next year." In that scenario, showing competence means sticking to an exercise regimen and a diet. When we lose competence by stopping our exercise regimen or falling off our diet, we create an excuse for ourselves ("I deserved a day off," "I was out late," "It was a party," etc.).

When we embrace compassion for ourselves, we immerse in full. A "diet" becomes a "nutrition plan," and we think bigger and more broadly about it. An "exercise plan" becomes a "lifestyle choice." The beauty of this language is that you don't have to make an excuse for yourself any longer. Why? Because an excuse is decidedly different than an explanation. This is the language that feels right—and it is the language we have tried to adopt within the framework of compassion.

A compassionate parent raising compassionate children inherently knows their children are fully immersed in their own lives. There is quite obviously a reason they did not take out the trash—and we want to know what the explanation is, because it will help us to fully know them better.

If we are truly in this realm of compassion together, our children also need an explanation from the parent about why it is important. Let's be honest, trash is a trivial thing. What about underage drinking, drug use, or sex? Those are not so trivial, and a compassionate parent will want to have explanation-based conversations with their kids early rather than excuse-based conversations late.

Explanation-based conversations allow us to be more proactive, more involved, more open, and more connected. The wonderful thing about kids is that they are so flexible. You do not need to tell them you are changing the language frameworks and conversational paradigms; you just do it. As stated in the introduction, the language change is the easy part. The thinking frameworks and internal dialogue are far more important and difficult.

Likewise, compassionate managers want to hear explanations because they care for and are fully immersed with their employees, and they realize excuses are counterproductive to everyone's goals.

Deep down, employees want to feel valued—and as leaders, we want our employees to feel valued, to feel heard from, and to work with passion. We want to reduce turnover. The only way to get there is through culture, and every good leader knows this. An excuse culture will not be one that earns a place on the "best places to work" list. An explain culture is one where employees feel heard, valued, and committed. This language paradigm allows us to walk away from the constant judging, evaluation, and polarity that exist in so many workplaces.

As we wrote in the introduction, people are not afraid of being wrong. They are afraid of being blamed. There are countless tools available that permit stakeholders (both internal and external) to assess areas to grow and measure how they are being successful.

In an influential 2013 article about the best way for new leaders to build trust, veteran software CEO Jim Dougherty stated, "Establishing trust is *the* top priority. Whether you are taking over a small department, an entire division, a company, or even a Boy Scout troop, the first thing you must get is the trust of the members of that entity. When asked, most leaders will agree to this notion, but few do anything to act on it" (para. 5).

The trust gap is a real thing for most organizations and nearly all workplace relationships. Further, in launching their widely adopted "The Leadership Practices Inventory" in 2003, James M. Kouzes and Barry Z. Posner wrote, "Leadership is a reciprocal relationship between those who choose to lead and those who choose to follow. Any discussion of leadership must attend to the dynamics of this relationship" (p. 1). There is a connection between credibility, trust, and leadership effectiveness. A leader who is immersed in competence-based evaluations has to work much harder to establish credibility and trust—and often they do not achieve them.

A gut check is not the same thing as a sucker punch. In your closest relationships, is there a trust gap? More pointedly, are you creating and maintaining systems and structures in your sphere of influence that are actively creating a trust gap? Establishing trust is a leadership mandate.

The Problem with Trust

A final thought about the word "trust." It seems nearly everyone talks about having trust, building trust, losing trust, etc. We are quickly losing interest in this word, as it is both overused and misunderstood. Trusting in organizations and trusting in leadership are starting to carry tremendous negative connotations because trust is something "earned," which brings value-laden judgement language, landing us squarely into the competence leadership paradigm.

Trust as a word and paradigm forces us to think of strong and weak leadership, which conjures up value judgments of good and bad. Instead of trust, we encourage you to embrace "unconditional faith." We want to have unconditional faith in those we work with. We want unconditional faith in our organization's commitment to excellence. Deep down, we don't want others to have trust in us ... we want them to have unconditional faith in our integrity, character, and leadership.

Faith is permanent, immovable, unshakable belief, and it is oriented toward purpose. Trust is temporal, convenient, and easily broken. Maybe trust isn't right for you either. If you are like us and aspire to unconditional faith over trust, you must commit to compassionate leadership.

And Then There Is Failure ...

A threat to nearly every business is the fear of disruptive innovation. Harvard Business School Professor Clayton Christenson, an expert on disruptive innovation, mapped this territory well. Countless books are available to help us to recognize and prepare for disruptive innovation. An industry that is soon to be disrupted is one that will be making an excuse at a future date. With all the literature available, why is it that so many companies still struggle with innovation?

Creating a culture where people are encouraged to explore and think on their own sounds great, and we see examples throughout the country and the world. Over nearly two decades, we have been looking at what all these companies have in common—and as elementary as this might sound, we never see examples of excuses, but we do see lots of examples of explanations. Just make a mental list of companies that have made excuses in the past five or ten years. How many have gone out of business or are struggling? There is obviously much more language that goes along with what helps a company to thrive, but the explanation language is a key foundational element.

What does this mean for the climate you are creating today, which will become your culture and eventually your policy? Compassionate leadership allows us to fully embrace "failure" by putting a number of small, calculated risks and investments into new solutions for our problems. We know many of these may falter, but some will become pathways to growth—think of it as stumbling forward. When this climate manifests as culture and is enacted as policy, it might sound something like this: "At [your industry here], we reduce the cost of failure while increasing the value." This is a powerful, risk-taking, compassionate culture that can only exist away from a risk-avoidant competent culture.

To embrace this struggle for compassionate leadership, we have to willingly share information and seek out explanations about areas of improvement, potential threats, areas of exposure, etc. Asking employees for explanations about what interests them, what questions they have, and what solutions they might offer opens the door to rich conversations about the future and often forestalls the need for an excuse later because "We didn't see it coming."

Let's turn our attention to our local surroundings and the organizations that make a community thrive. Think about local parent-teacher associations, city governments, faith-based groups, civic supporters, etc. We have all heard about their rapid decline in membership. We want to touch briefly on it here and come back again in future chapters. There are numerous reasons people are self-selecting out of these organizations, and one of them is because they regularly face difficult decisions. The world is becoming more complex, especially with technology tools, instant access to information, and social media. The competence framework puts us all in a position to be judged by what we say and what we do. It becomes far easier to neither say nor do anything. That way, we will not be judged.

A compassionate leader recognizes we cannot stonewall the decisions we are faced with, but at the same time we cannot be judged on our competence, because we will almost inevitably find ourselves in a position where we will make an excuse if we are wrong.

Practice Reframing Excuse Conversations

I want to introduce you to the phrase "accidental adversaries." It is important to be deft at knowing the value of paced decision-making and how to recognize that our decisions have consequences. A good way to think of this is recognizing the ball will always bounce more than one time. Anyone can tell you how the ball will bounce on first impact. Good leaders can predict the second, third, and fourth bounces.

Practice pausing before a conversation and say something like, "I don't want to become accidental adversaries down the road, so let me talk this through a little bit." Sharing an explanation early in the process of considering possible outcomes means we can circle back and not have to come up with an excuse later on. Using the language of accidental adversaries is something we have wholeheartedly adopted as part of our explanation framework.

Here's another phrase that has become part of our new language: "It's not a question *if* what you did matters to me, it's a question if *how* you did it matters to you." When we say this, we can immediately dismiss judgment from the conversation and talk about process. If you just marked that phrase with a highlighter or underlined it because you've set a goal to introduce it tomorrow, we'd like to pause and ask you to consider whether you have been laying the groundwork first. This phrase will fall flat if it comes from a competency manager. It will offend. It will be immediately disingenuous. A compassionate leader, on the other hand, can use this language from a place of honest inquiry and unconditional faith. If people in your workplace are generally wrongdoers and you are the "police," this is not the phrase for you.

Let's also be honest and stay connected to reality. Will we make mistakes as leaders of our organizations? Most certainly.

As much as we try to avoid them, we all make mistakes. It's inevitable.

Within your organization, listen for phrases like "the unintended consequences of our decisions," because this is simply another way of saying excuses within a competence framework. At first, you will probably find other excuse language throughout your organization. Part of the culture-busting work that needs to happen is first recognizing the thumbprint of excuses in our everyday language.

Crucial Conversations: Tools for Talking When the Stakes Are High and *Crucial Accountability: Tools for Resolving Violated Expectations, Broken Commitments, and Bad Behavior* are two books that were influential in our journey and continue to deeply resonate with us. After reading them, although we were still operating within a competence leadership model, we made more progress moving away from it thanks to new techniques and skills that helped us set the stage for and successfully complete game-changing conversations.

Let's think forward for a moment. When is the next interaction you are likely to have where an excuse is bound to rear its ugly head? Is it a missed deadline or an unmet goal you are hesitant to address? You have an excuse conversation in your calendar somewhere lurking for you, I can guarantee it. How you prepare for it is a decision point for you.

TRANSFORMATIONAL LEADERSHIP IN PRACTICE

MARCUS SOUTRA

President, Eye to Eye

After Marcus Soutra was identified with ADHD and dyslexia as a young child, he came to understand that he was different from many of his classmates. This early experience became part of his identity as an individual, and as he got older, he was struck by the fact that students with learning disabilities are often destined to fail in school before they get the support they need.

As Marcus headed off to college, he began considering how to support other students with learning differences. "I came to the conclusion that we have a very broken education system," he said. "It's incredibly inequitable for students who learn differently. They don't know how to advocate for themselves. They don't know what they need, and they often feel stigmatized."

The culmination of all these experiences and feelings led to a decision to pursue education and become a teacher. "I thought I would use my dyslexia as a way of understanding students and having more empathy for them," he shared. "I quickly realized that my story was an incredibly valuable tool in the classroom. I was able to change the culture of the classroom to reach students."

As a young student teacher in New Hampshire, Marcus was extremely curious about the transformation he had created within his own classroom, and he was exhilarated by the thought of scaling a culture where students were encouraged to embrace their learning differences and ask for help. He began to explore different models that could work on a broader scale. "Serendipitously, a professor approached me and said, 'You know, there's a guy named David Flink, and he's at Brown University right now, and he's running a mentoring program that's aimed at the same things that you're trying to accomplish.'"

The two ended up meeting, and they got right to work, partnering to create Eye to Eye, a national mentoring nonprofit organization that empowers young people with learning differences.

The Importance of Shared Leadership

Since that opportune meeting, Marcus has learned a great deal about leadership and collaboration. He strongly believes in valuing shared leadership and dismantling the myth of the lone hero.

"I think the idea of a lone hero entrepreneur can really be a lie," he said. "It's about a team. It's about a collaboration among many people in different roles lifting the work up and getting it done."

Marcus is adamant about this idea because when he was in college, he had a very unusual student teaching experience that transformed his belief in the importance of leveraging and promoting shared leadership. "Right off the bat, on the very first day of student teaching, the classroom teacher and I sat at the front of the room together, and we were introduced to the students as joint teachers. This was very unusual—and not something my fellow colleagues were experiencing—but we were both viewed as leaders to the students. I still remember that day and the impact it had on me very vividly, and I try to remember that and model the same approach with my team."

Fostering a Learning Culture

Marcus asks everyone he interviews for a job at Eye to Eye the same question: How do you learn? He listens to understand the rationale behind how they answer the question, because he believes it's very valuable to know that aspect of ourselves.

But Eye to Eye takes this knowledge even further. The organization has developed what you might call a work IEP, personalizing how each person learns and communicates most effectively. "Students have an IEP in school to help the teacher understand their strengths or weaknesses," Marcus explained, "and we work with our staff to try to understand how we each receive communication best and in what form."

As a leader, Marcus knows it's his job to help inform strategy, communicate the work of the organization, and drive revenue. But most importantly, he understands that he needs to live the values of the organization and center the work around the mission. This means living and breathing its values—and one of the ways he does this is by fostering a learning culture. For Marcus, this means intimately understanding everyone's reason for doing the work and their own personal mission for joining the organization.

"Some people come to Eye to Eye because their child has a learning difference, and they want to make the world better for them. Some people do it because they have a learning difference themselves. There are always very different answers to that question, but it's really, really important for us to get at the heart of why each individual team member is showing up."

Marcus has invested a great deal of time in helping Eye to Eye's workforce understand that they are all on this learning journey together. "I think people often expect leaders to have all of the answers. And I think the vulnerability of saying 'I'm learning alongside of you' can go a long way to transform an organization into one filled with self-actualized learners."

To him, this is not just a value statement on the wall. "We truly all are on this constant learning journey together," he said. "We need to collect data from best practices in the field. We need to assess historical knowledge within our organization and understand what's going on within the industry and in schools and how cultures are shifting. It's one thing to say that we are a learner-centered organization or an organization that values learning, but it's very different when you make that show up in every aspect of the work."

Operate from the Assumption of Best Intentions

Marcus believes that creating effective relationships with teams begins with building relationships. "Yes, what we're doing is work, but it still needs to be somewhat fun, and we need to be able to operate from the assumption of best intentions. Ideally you can get to the place where you can ask, 'Okay, why didn't that happen?' or 'How can we get this better next time?'"

To Marcus, operating from an assumption of best intentions means that if someone misses an email, for example, and their supervisor doesn't know why, they can either assume the employee simply forgot to do it, was really busy, or had something else get in the way—rather than assuming they are just lazy or they don't care about their work. "To do that," he said, "we need to make sure that we create that space to really get to know each other authentically. That's so important, and it takes time."

Marcus admitted that without a commitment to consistently invest in building relationships, the interpersonal work can get lost in the everyday demands of other tasks. To address this, he has come up with a couple of ways to maintain its status as a priority at Eye to Eye. "We literally list a personal check-in on the agenda for the first five or ten minutes of our meetings," he said. "Or I will ask my team how they are feeling on a scale of one to ten, both personally and professionally. That helps me instantly better understand where they are coming from."

And, he continued, when something does go awry, as it always will, individuals are encouraged to take a moment to celebrate those failures in what they call a joyous funeral. "If you begin a debrief about a challenging situation or an analysis for a loss from a place of vulnerability and compassion," he explained, "it's possible to have a learning moment and then be able to build from it and move on."

The Five Key Ingredients That Make It All Work

Marcus has distilled his approach at Eye to Eye into five words representing the key components that make the culture successful:

1. Empathy
2. Passion
3. Vulnerability
4. Autonomy
5. Listening.

"I think that listening in is something that people kind of underestimate," he said. "To be a good leader, listening to people and trying to understand who they are and trying to work with them to be able to maximize their gifts as a team member is so important."

CHAPTER 3

FROM ACCOUNTABILITY TO EMPOWERMENT, FEEDBACK TO FEEDFORWARD

Now that we're feeling more comfortable with the concept of excuse versus explain, the next step of our journey is a movement away from accountability. About 10 years ago, Sarah and I both grew tired of the language of accountability, which is almost exclusively a language of competence. This is language that separates people and does not bring them together. We don't like having our competence called into question, and we don't want to work with people we have to hold accountable. Accountability most certainly will not create unconditional faith, either.

In the early days of the study of effective leaders, we all became enamored with becoming data driven. Collecting data, scrutinizing data, managing data, sharing data became part of our lexicon. "What gets measured gets done" grew into a mantra of sorts.

It was exactly the right thing to do at the time, but we've grown beyond being data driven. When the idea of collecting data to drive performance was new, leaders throughout the world adopted a language around data-driven concepts. As stated previously, this language created a self-serving paradigm that defined both climate and culture and led to policies and governance that supported a data-driven culture of accountability. We started to measure outcomes in terms of accountability to shareholders, stakeholders, and managers. The idea was that accountability as a consequence would lead to success as an antecedent. The problem: It doesn't actually work.

We can hold people and organizations accountable all day long, but when does it guarantee success? The honest answer is never. As a theory (and accountability-based leadership is a theory of improvement), if accountability led to success, then everywhere we put accountability in place, success would follow.

A theory is a set of ideas that explains facts or events. If a theory is plausible and scientifically acceptable, it is often perceived as a universally applicable "truth." Accountability as a leadership truth would be something that guarantees improvement or success—but we have tens of thousands (if not millions) of examples where holding someone accountable didn't actually lead to success or even improvement.

Let's use your physical health as an example. Let's assume you are not in the best shape of your life. Let's also imagine that we tell you we will hold you accountable six months from now if you don't improve your physical health. Will that cause you to improve? Not necessarily. It depends. Is the accountability tied to a reward or a punishment? Is the reward enough to make you change, or is the punishment strong enough to inspire change?

Both rewards and punishments are at the heart of accountability tools. They reinforce competence language, power structures, and established political hierarchy. A compassionate, transformative leader who intends real change recognizes this as being counterproductive.

Eliminating the Need for Accountability

Yet accountability is upheld at the deepest levels of all our organizations. You will find the language of accountability everywhere. Once the bell of accountability has been rung, you can't unring it.

Are we suggesting we move away from accountability? No, we're suggesting we reframe the conversation to eliminate the need for accountability altogether.

Think of accountability in the form of a verbal equation. In our organizations, something plus something else plus another thing equals success and accountability. Accountability is always on the outcome side of the equation. The "formula" only makes sense in one direction: moving toward accountability at the end. *Did you accomplish the goal or not?* In that regard, feedback is a necessary component because it is always backward-looking—which is great if you're driving backward.

So how can we collectively walk away from accountability by eliminating the need for accountability?

We have to add something to the front end of the equation. Something that is forward-looking. That something is empowerment. If we put empowerment and responsibility at the front and have an honest and compassionate (using the definition "to suffer with") conversation around responsibility, the need for accountability disappears. As a manager, having a conversation about "How will you show empowerment for the goal/outcome?" lays the groundwork for growth metrics, outcome measures, etc. These are the same as the measures of accountability, but when they're framed in the language of empowerment, they have a different feeling. More importantly, their impact within your organization will be profound.

Feedback to Feedforward

In order to make this leap from accountability to empowerment, you also have to abandon feedback. The word is imbued with backward-looking judgement criteria and competency-based assessments. Some people have tried to rebrand the word, but the word itself is the problem. It has fifty-plus years of history loaded within it. Collectively, we do our organizations a big favor by eliminating feedback (showing people who they are) and embracing feedforward (showing people who they are becoming).

To close the loop on the health example, once a person takes full responsibility for their health, there is no need for follow-up accountability or feedback. Being responsible for yourself, and to yourself, means you will always choose a realistic nutrition plan, a balanced perspective on the importance of exercise, and a realization that your suffering is part of a compassionate lifestyle. Frankly, it is a far more effective framework for personal success. As a theory, responsibility always works far better than accountability.

Consider your current policies, evaluation documents, HR office initiatives, reports, and goals. How much is framed in the language of accountability and feedback? We're guessing most, or maybe all. This is a good time to stop and think about the monumental task in front of you if you are committed to this new language of leadership. What feedback and accountability frameworks are currently getting in the way of effective leadership?

So, if we are not going to be data driven, how should we be talking about data? For me, the shift was moving away from data driven to data informed. We like to use health analogies, as you have already discovered, so we will use another one here. Many people use fitness tracker apps on their phones or devices attached to their wrists. There are stories of people who take this data to the extreme in measuring their sleep, steps, miles, and exercises. Some become so data driven it becomes counterproductive to their health, causing more stress and contributing to an unhealthy relationship with nutrition and exercise. These outliers are a wonderful case study in taking data-driven behavior to the extreme. Many people can use these fitness apps and trackers in an effective way, and their actions are not data driven but rather data informed.

Being data driven to the extreme in an organization is likewise an unhealthy relationship with information—and is ultimately detrimental to an organization's well-being.

Using information to make decisions is being data informed. It gives us the opportunity to back away from the data and not let it be the judgement-defining, competence-oriented monster it has become for so many people. Being data informed means that we have learned some things because of our data, but, if we are being honest with ourselves, we probably have more questions than answers.

This is a decidedly good thing for any organization. Questions and inquiry lead to new ideas, creativity, and innovation. Data should always create more questions, not answers. As you think about your organization's association with data, it is best to ask the question very simply. We have always believed we can identify your data culture using language we all learned in kindergarten: Is your data culture "hide and seek" or "show and tell"? If yours is a culture of hide and seek, you have work to do. Hide-and-seek data cultures are built on competence, excuses, accountability, low morale, and low engagement. A show-and-tell data culture is always built on responsibility, compassion, inquiry, growth, and creativity.

There are other unintended consequences to the accountability language paradigm. In education, we have especially fallen prey to the D.R.I.P. Syndrome (an acronym for Data Rich and Information Poor). We became entrenched in the language of accountability so quickly that we started collecting data on anything and everything we could to "prove" we were doing a good job. The problem was that we were full of data but had no real information about how to improve education. It became an effort to collect data for the sake of collecting data. This is decidedly unhelpful for everyone—and counter-productive for real and sustainable improvement.

A Four-Part Framework for Transformational Leadership

This is a book about deep transformational leadership. To that end, a Langston University (2016) paper entitled "Transformational Leadership" describes it as "a leadership approach that causes change in individuals and social systems. In its ideal form, it creates valuable and positive change in the followers with the end goal of developing followers into leaders. Enacted in its authentic form, transformational leadership enhances the motivation, morale, and performance of followers" (p. 1).

We think it is important to add this is not specific to "top-down" leadership. Transformational leaders can be found anywhere in the hierarchy of an organization. Some of the best leadership we have witnessed falls in the "leading-up" category.

Here is a four-part framework that lays out the essence of transformational leadership:

1. **Communicating the "why" of our work.** This is the rationale. An ethical connection to the purpose. As we have in the first three chapters, we will continue to articulate why this change in leadership language is important. We don't take for granted that you know our "why," which is the reason we have made it a central part of our writing. Embracing your "why" for doing this work is mission critical for your success. Without a meaningful why, your words will fall flat, and your success is in jeopardy. We have told you our "why" ... what's yours?

2. **Communicating the "who" of the work.** This builds unconditional faith and an ability to connect with the emotions of others. For this book, our "who" is you. We are sharing stories of personal and

professional development in the hopes that you can visualize yourself on this path. For our organizations, the "who" are the people who work there (including Sarah and me). We have to be crystal clear who will do the work if we intend transformative change. Who will do this work of changing the language of leadership in your organization?

3. **Communicating the "how" of the work.** Taking an empowerment stance, we might take this communication a step further and co-design the work. We have shared some stories along our learning path, but you will chart your own. How you go from where you are to where you want to be is important. You must have the compassion to treat others as professionals in their work. Investing in training, resources, and processes is non-negotiable.

   We will write more about this in subsequent chapters and help illuminate language that often causes barriers in our organizations. Communicating the "how" of our work means enthusiastically embracing new ideas. By doing so, we can reduce the cost of failure while increasing the value. This is a powerful paradigm shift for any culture. You must be willing to immerse yourself fully in the work and dreams of others if you intend to embrace compassionate leadership to the fullest.

4. **Communicating the "what" of our work.** We are making specific requests of you. This is work you must do to make transformative change happen in your organization. Improvement cannot exist in a vacuum, and we must communicate the "what" of our work tactfully and with deep compassion.

Let's take a moment and share an evolution in thinking and theory about why compassionate language works. Everything in the world of competence is a judgement of good or bad. Put more directly, competence is a judgement of "strong" or "weak." If you are strong in sales, you are in the competent framework. You can go from strong to weak in the blink of an eye or over months and/or years. You can be weak and get strong, but you are still rooted in competence. Strong and weak assume that you are fragile. If you are strong, you are fragile to becoming weak, and if you are weak, you are fragile to becoming obsolete.

We highly recommend the work of Nassim Nicholas Talib, who has written mostly in the field of economics around becoming "antifragile." If strong/weak is fragile, we want to create environments where we are antifragile. Antifragile requires us to shed ourselves of the frameworks of competence and arrive at a deeper state where we are no longer subject to the construct of fragile. We do not want our employees, our organizations, or ourselves as individuals to exist in a fragile state—and yet nearly everything in our organizations reinforces fragility.

The work in front of us is hard, to be sure, but we think we speak for every leader when we say we want to be antifragile, or immune against strong/weak value judgments.

TRANSFORMATIONAL LEADERSHIP IN PRACTICE

KIMBERLY SMITH

Executive Director of the Center for Inclusive Innovation and the League of Innovative Schools, Digital Promise

Just a few years ago, Kimberly Smith was engaged to a wonderful man, planning a beautiful October wedding for 200 people, and enjoying a rewarding career.

She could never have anticipated what would happen on a midsummer day in 2016. Her fiancé, George, died unexpectedly. Losing her fiancé far too early was life shattering. So many hopes, dreams, and plans for the future were wiped away in a moment. "That experience ... it turned me inside out," Kimberly shared.

But strange things happen through suffering. Throughout the last five years, while navigating through her grief, Kimberly experienced her own revelation. "There is no longer a distinction between who I am and what I do," she said.

"I feel even more clarity now about my soul mission, which is at the intersection of how I live my life and how I engage in the work I do," she continued, "and I have been pushing education leaders, including myself, to be different and to show up differently, especially for students who are furthest from opportunity."

Breaking the Fourth Wall

Throughout the past few years, Kimberly has focused on her personal "why" and how this drives her career at Digital Promise, where she strives to increase innovation in K-12 education. This has led her to continuously "find the humanity in the work."

"When I was in TV production classes in college, we would talk about this notion of breaking the fourth wall," she said. The fourth wall is an imaginary boundary that separates the story from the real world. This term comes from the theater, where the three surrounding walls enclose the stage while an invisible fourth wall is left out for the sake of the viewer. This is the screen viewers watch, which is like a one-way mirror. The audience can see and comprehend the story, but the story cannot comprehend the existence of the audience.

"Breaking the fourth wall is how we reach that deeply personal space where you dive below the surface level," Kimberly said. "Now, with the pandemic, you see in my home, you know me personally, and you know what I'm going through—and what ends up happening is that everything equalizes at that point. You no longer have the separate 'work self.' You no longer have this idea that leaders have certain types of lives, and I just think it's really powerful because you begin to see a new humanity in people, one rooted in a deep compassion that creates this overlapping connection to the work you do."

Kimberly feels that if her personal and professional worlds are not intersecting, then her work is no longer true to who she is. Her hope is that a deep compassion is emerging for other leaders as well. "I hope people are leading from a place of not just a professional perspective, but they're also bringing themselves into their work."

The Competency Conundrum

When it comes to data about student growth and success, the first question Kimberly likes to ask herself—and her team the Center for Inclusive Innovation and the League of Innovative Schools, where she is executive director—is "What is the outcome that data is not showing us?"

At the Center, the focus is on the outcomes *and* the process underneath. "That's a very different way of looking at the work," Kimberly noted. "It's not just about the outcome of the student and how they scored on a mathematics test, but it's the process as well. When you think of those two together, it gives you a different view, because if you're evaluating the learning process and the students' experience in the learning process in addition to the outcomes, you can see a much a broader picture of what's truly going on."

Concentrating 100 percent on the data, she believes, distracts from the humanity of the student. "If you only focus on the data, you just shut down the creative learning process, the creative learning space, and the ability to understand what's happening along the journey instead of just at the end result of that journey," she said.

Since launching in 2020, the Center has explored this approach to data, particularly as it relates to equity. "We realize there is a process in how we understand equity and whether or not equitable conditions are taking shape," Kimberly said. "We are continually collecting feedback on the experience throughout the process so that in the end we can determine if the process did net the outcomes we were expecting. It's a new intention to have those run side-by-side to each other."

Creating Transformation Together

Kimberly believes that work culture, transformation, and change cannot solely begin with leaders. Instead, the Center emphasizes co-designing its culture together as an organization. "Transformational leaders roll up their sleeves with teams to design the culture together," she said. "Right now, we're working on a Center charter, which is going to be about our equity commitments and our core values, and it's important that doesn't come from just one person or one leader, but all of us. I do think that's how you set the stage for a collaborative culture, because everyone is part of the transformation as you co-design a culture together."

To take this even further, Kimberly said, she invites every member of her team to pursue one audacious goal. "When people start working with me, I always ask them what's the biggest thing they want to accomplish in the role that will create change? And then I want to support them as much as I can in making that thing happen. To me, that's feedforward."

Fortunately for Kimberly and her team, Digital Promise is entrepreneurial and design centric, which creates room for people to shape a big goal aligned with the organizational North Star. "I encourage people to focus less on a specific pathway and more on the biggest, most audacious thing they can do here."

Kimberly has seen this strategy work, including with her former communications lead, who wanted to launch a comprehensive portal for districts to showcase their innovation stories. She achieved that big goal—and then went on to her next big goal of attending the Harvard Graduate School of Education.

"In my career," Kimberly reflected, "one of the things that I've probably done well is to identify the biggest levers and opportunities for change and then push to accomplish what I could, and I want to support others to do the same."

Pulling It All Together

If there's one thing Kimberly would share about compassion, it is that it's not easy. "It takes effort and intention, and it can't come without building relationships and tapping into someone's 'why,'" she said. "It can't come without being invested in and building a culture that is going to be an expression of interconnectedness. We spend at least 40 hours a week with these people, and relationships take shape within this system that we call an organization. If we focus on finding the humanity in the work we do, then talent, heart, and love will survive and thrive throughout our organizations."

CHAPTER 4

FROM SOFT SKILLS TO POWER SKILLS

In the field of education, we have fallen into the language of "soft skills." You've heard the phrase and probably said it yourself. Soft skills first found their origin in 1972, when they were described as in a leadership report for the U.S. Army as "important job-related skills that involve little or no interaction with machines and whose application on the job is quite generalized." The definition has evolved in the past forty years to include just about any set of personality traits that allow a person to build an effective working relationship with another.

This is another example of a definition which was exactly right ... for the time period. In 1972, personal technology (cell phones, laptops, tech networks, social media) simply did not exist. The idea of hard skills was vitally important, and the idea of soft skills was appropriate. However, we assert that the paradigm has largely outlived its usefulness.

Soft skills as a phrase suggests there is something soft in working on relationships and connecting with people, while the "hard" work happens in the digital realm. Because we have become so technologically oriented as a society, it just does not make sense to think of these as hard skills anymore. Any nine-year-old can teach themselves basic programming and networking skills.

More and more, employers are crying out for employees with soft skills. With each passing year, employees (and leaders) are getting worse with soft skills, and I don't think this is a coincidence. Moreover, the longer we all keep talking about soft skills, the worse the situation will get.

How can these soft skills be bad things? It's not that the skills per se are bad. Rather, the language we use is failing us. Why would these skills be considered soft? The value judgement of "soft" leads us to believe they are somehow less important, an afterthought or nice addition to the "real work" we should be doing.

We advocate abandoning the language of soft skills forever. This phrase needs to be buried along with other phrases we have been describing in this book. We believe soft skills have truly become power skills in our current society. Across all industries, those who excel demonstrate they are able to form strong human connections with others. They know how to shake hands (and why it's important). They know how to look others in the eye, speak articulately, converse on the phone, carry themselves in public, and inspire others. They are personally charismatic and at ease in a variety of settings. (Later in the book, we'll talk more about the power these skills bring to networking.)

But first, we'd like to emphasize this important point: Hard skills and soft skills are the language of competence. They are about fragility. There is a place for hard skills in every industry. They can be judged, evaluated, and assessed. Virtually every hard skill lives in the paradigm of competence. Competence is not evil, and hard skills are important. Hard skills are something that can be managed. Power skills, however, live in the world of the compassionate organization. Power skills have become the new language of leadership. This is the evolution.

'What I Want for You'

With power skills in mind, let's return to the topic of building trust. Writing in the *Research Management Review* in 2014, consultant David Mineo explained his view that "[t]rust is the glue that binds the leader to her/his followers and provides the capacity for organizational and leadership success" (p. 1). This explanation is important—and hopefully your mind immediately unpacks that definition of building trust as competence and strong/weak based. Soft skills within the trust framework guarantee we will build policies and procedures that ultimately fall prey to a fragile definition of trust. Juxtapose hard/soft skills with power skills and you immediately move to the framework of antifragile, compassionate leadership and organizational strength.

A very wise friend of mine coined a phrase that captures this concept brilliantly. Dessalen Wood, an innovative HR executive, shared this phrase with me several years ago, and when I heard it, I knew she had embraced compassionate leadership. When she speaks about her people, she talks about the difference between what I need from you versus what I want for you.

Think about this for a moment. How many times have you told your people, "This is what I need from you"? We have all said or implied this phrase. Maybe even daily. Reflect on your cadre of direct reports or your boss. How many times have you told them what you need from them?

If you use this language, you are living in a world of the fragile. You are living your commitment to competence. You will almost certainly never get your followers' very best work. When a board tells the leader what they need, they are sending the covert message that the leader is not doing their best work. They are overtly sending the message that there will be judgement. They are encouraging leaders to do the same with their employees, and this will ultimately create power structures, policies, and procedures grounded in competence.

It's easy to understand this in relation to children. If you tell them what you need from them, you are not asking them to think autonomously, to take responsibility, or to become the agents of their own lives. Every parent has all told their kids what they need from them. When I look back on how I have talked with my own children, I think back to such moments as missed opportunities. This is true for our work environments as well.

A far better approach with employees, your own boss or board, and, for that matter, your children is a conversation that focuses on what you want for them. I want for my children (and employees and leaders) to have a meaningful experience. I want for them to have agency in their lives. I want for them to have deep relationships with others. I want for them to feel they are making a real impact in the lives of others.

Unfortunately, many of us have never told our employees what we wanted for them. Once I embraced this evolution to compassionate leadership, this is all I talked about! For me, this started with the board. I encouraged this to be a two-way dialogue. I told them what I wanted for them and asked them to tell me what they wanted for me.

This conversation was the epitome of vulnerability, and it led to one of the best conversations I've ever had with a board of directors. We spoke honestly about goals and connected compassionately in a way that is hard to describe. During that same conversation, I also told them what I wanted from myself. I shared that I wanted to do the best work of my life. I wanted to grow our organization to be the best in the region, state, and country. I told them they don't need to judge or punish, because I will do plenty of that on my own.

I did not need their accountability or competence judgments or good/bad dichotomies because they wouldn't lead me to do my best work. I shared the internal suffering (be compassionate with yourself first) and that led me to connect my compassion to their compassion. In that space and during that conversation, we became an antifragile team.

You can then take what you learn and bring it forward to your leadership teams. Have the courage to say you will never again tell them what you want from them. Forevermore, assume they want to do their best work, and explain that your job is to help them through the struggle.

If you resist the temptation to tell them what you want from them but share what you want for them, it will change the working dynamics in seconds.

This does not mean we should never talk about outcomes or goals. Of course we will talk about this a lot with our teams—but not in the space of expectations, accountability, or competence. Instead, we can talk about goals and outcomes in relation to responsibility and in terms of what we want for them.

This slight language change is a linchpin for teams evolving away from competence leadership and more fully into compassionate leadership. Incidentally, in the Victoria

Independent School District, our success by virtually every measure was superior to anything we had achieved prior to that conversation. We truly moved away from fragility as a team and organization and began on our path to antifragility. And when your team/organization moves to antifragile, nothing is impossible. Every goal becomes imminently achievable, because the team bonds. Members take responsibility for each other. It's the super fuel you have been looking for in your organization.

The question is, are you vulnerable enough to have the conversation? It is an odd juxtaposition that embracing your vulnerability is what makes you antifragile.

The movement towards what we want for our employees brings with it a shift in thinking about mentorship. We have all had the great fortune of mentoring other leaders, and all of us take pride in the role of traditional mentor. You no doubt mentor early career leaders—and when doing so, you likely focus on competence. We strongly believe early career leaders need to demonstrate competence in order to build credibility.

However, as we've emphasized throughout this book, your evolution in leadership will mean an evolution in thinking. The shift from competence to compassion requires a change in thinking about mentoring as well. It is incumbent upon us to move away from mentoring and towards sponsorship.

In mentoring, you give of your time and knowledge. With sponsorship, you give your time, knowledge, power, and insight ... in other words, you give your whole self. Mentoring builds trust. Sponsorship provides unconditional faith. Sponsorship is obviously a deeper connection, and with it comes a more powerful experience. Here's another way to think about the choice before you: Do you want to be thought of as a competent mentor or a compassionate sponsor?

There Really Is No Choice for Us

Today is your day to embrace these power skills with your teams and your bosses. The power skills you are acquiring are allowing you to open up more deeply than you ever have. You can now live squarely in the world without judgement or the fear of becoming weak, without focusing on your people only when it is convenient.

By focusing on what you want for others, as opposed to what you want from them, you will have unlocked new potential in yourself and those with whom you work. If you think about your current organization and realize you have much work in front of you, that is fantastic news! You get to start today on a new path. This path will give more meaning to your work and allow for the deepest connections you have yet experienced with others.

And when you are judged (and we promise you will be judged), remember, those who judge you are demanding your obedience because they have a privileged view of reality, and they are requiring you to subordinate to their view. This is the highest form of competence and value judgement. Embrace their suffering—without accepting it.

TRANSFORMATIONAL LEADERSHIP IN PRACTICE

ASEEM GIRI

Head of Content, Robin

Aseem Giri began his career in investment banking on Wall Street at Salomon Brothers, where his aspirations centered around going into private equity and eventually managing his own hedge fund. "I've always had this entrepreneurial spirit, so I moved to California, and I worked my way up to partner in the fund. Eventually, I left to launch my own fund that was largely made up of Southeast Asian capital based in Singapore, and I ran that for a few years."

Aseem's goals, however, came to a screeching halt in a split second when his son was unexpectedly diagnosed with a rare blood disease called Severe Aplastic Anemia when he was just two-and-a-half years old.

"I've deliberated on every decision in my life. Do I go into this profession? Do I attend this university? Do I marry this woman? The decision to drop everything and focus on my son's health was the clearest decision I've ever made," Aseem said. "I felt I had one chance to save him, and I could always make money later in life. It also helped that being the son of an immigrant family, I was always in the habit of saving, so when I did well financially in my 20s, I banked a lot of it. That provided me with flexibility when I wasn't able to work for a number of years, and I could still provide for my family."

Thankfully, today Aseem's son is cured after having undergone multiple bone marrow transplants. "The fact that he's still with me is the most important, precious thing," he said. "I didn't know if that was going to be the case at the time."

Sadly, Aseem lost his mother to lung cancer during that same difficult time. "My parents had moved to Maryland," he recalled, "and my son's second bone marrow transplant was at the National Institute of Health in Bethesda. I will never forget November and December of 2012. I was with my son in the mornings and with my mother in the afternoons at Washington Hospital Center."

After his son's health improved, Aseem made another key decision: He did not want to go back to running a fund. "It sounds very glamorous, but your hours are not really yours. You travel a lot. You have bosses in your limited partners or your investors. So I made a conscious decision to become an entrepreneur." Aseem's family-related interest in the health and wellness industry led him to started and then sell three health and wellness companies.

Then Aseem was introduced to Robin, a company that connects K-12 students and teachers with mental health coaches to build their social-emotional skills and work through life's toughest challenges. He was immediately captivated by the vision for bridging the health and wellness needs of students by connecting them with adults who have navigated similar challenges, helping to create a safe place for students to talk about their lives.

"I felt like there needed to be some modification in technology and platforms available to young people, but also a general willingness to talk about mental health and not have it be stigmatized," Aseem said. "I think that's finally shifted, in the last several years, and I think there's an openness now to talk about it—a willingness to talk about it. I was excited to be supporting this new vision with Robin."

Understanding the Whole Person (Even When It's Hard)

Aseem has often wondered if his leading with vulnerability and compassion might make it seem that he's someone who can be fooled. "There have been plenty of occasions when people see that about me and try to take advantage," he said. "But it still compels me to continue coming from that place."

Aseem seeks to understand the whole person. He doesn't see anyone who works with him as a number, and he doesn't have a narrow, myopic view of what they do. "Everybody comes to the table with their emotions and experiences. If you nurture and understand that, then you can really bring out the best in your people, make them feel comfortable, and enable them to become champions for your organization," he said. "I feel like I've just naturally always gravitated towards doing that."

Having this understanding helps Aseem see where people's strengths and abilities lie. "You just try and celebrate that," he said. "You give them ways that they can showcase it."

He believes the junior people in an organization can learn a lot about leadership through observation. He reminds them that "we have these other executives that you can look to as role models in terms of how they present ideas, build community, and bring team members together. I feel like that's one of the most effective ways to inspire young leaders to grow in a compassionate way."

Leading with Vulnerability

Aseem often deliberates the varying perspectives of authority. For instance, compare how school districts' partners and their high school students might view it based on their experiences and needs. "Authority comes from a number of places, and certainly the initials after a last name are important to district leaders and parents who are more impressed with titles and backgrounds," he acknowledged. "But to gain authority with adolescents, how you connect with them is the most important thing. If you have actually gone through what a teen is dealing with, that's how connection happens."

When Aseem supports Robin's mental health coaches with developing their workshops, he tries to tap into their personal stories to connect with the group. "One of our most successful coaches, Nyeesha Williams, is not afraid to be vulnerable, and she does it from a place of absolute love and understanding," he said. "When I met with Nyeesha, I read her book first, and I began quoting her poems back to her in our conversation. It created an incredibly strong bond between us."

Aseem acknowledges that at times it's difficult to know the right thing to say when others open up in response to your heightened vulnerability, but just listening can be what most people really want. "It's about 'Hey, I hear you, I see you, it's an unfortunate situation you're in, and I'm sorry.' It's okay to support your team members if they need time away from work, if they need mental health days, or if they can't get to something because a family member is having a health issue."

He brings this vulnerability home with him too. "I think it makes me a much better father," he added. "If someone approaches you or you approach someone to do something, whether it's your employee or as a member of your team, showing some compassion or understanding about what's going on in their lives can make all the difference."

CHAPTER 5

FROM WORK/LIFE TO LIFE/WORK

We have explored suffering for many pages now, and we hope you are getting a deeper sense of what suffering means for you. This is a good time to unpack it a bit more. Stop and think for a moment about something that is not going well or something that you have strong negative feelings about, as this next section won't work unless you have a really strong idea in mind.

What is it that's causing you these strong emotions, right now at this moment? The thing you are thinking about isn't right or wrong, per se, although it may seem like it. That perception is essentially caused by two things: 1) You have labeled something "right" or "wrong." 2) The thing you are thinking about doesn't align with how you think it should be.

In life, we almost always cause our own suffering. The shortcut to deeply understanding your suffering is the recognition you are not allowing the thing to be the way it is. Letting go of your suffering means letting go of your label and accepting the thing as it is.

We cannot reinforce this point enough: Suffering is self-imposed. Connecting by sharing it with someone else makes you tremendously vulnerable because that means openly admitting you have placed a value label on a thing. You are sharing your lenses, and sometimes this is a deeply personal experience.

After many years of compassionate leadership (suffering with others), we have come to realize many (if not most) people have countless unexamined lenses. People don't often realize they are placing value judgments on things they have strong opinions about and that they are causing their own suffering.

If you don't like your current health situation, you suffer. If you don't like how your neighbor is raising their children, you suffer. If you don't like how your employees are delivering results, you suffer. The point of this exercise is for you to realize these stories you are telling yourselves are not about your neighbors or your employees. You are simply revealing your personal lenses.

Compassion for yourself means recognizing when you suffer and understanding why. When you release your lens, you can more deeply connect with another through their suffering and help them realize the cause of their own suffering. This will be the most powerful, liberating, and transformative part of your leadership development.

A personal example of suffering follows, to help illustrate this point.

In my leadership evolution, I began to realize the whole work/life balance thing would never work for me. I came upon this realization very early in the process—and full credit goes to my children and wife.

As I embarked on my career as a school CEO, I worked really hard for success. While serving as a school district superintendent, I was also trying to finish a Ph.D., improve schools, speak at conferences, make connections with other leaders, and generally grow a career. I was gone so much that my wife was effectively a single parent. Family time was a Friday night football game, which I was mostly required to attend, but I tried to count that time as "double" when I invited my wife to the games to watch our children as I wandered about shaking hands and chatting with people. It was a recipe for disaster. Work/life balance was 99% work, 1% life.

Then it dawned on me that by thinking work/life, I was making it okay for work to be the most important thing in my life. When I wasn't working (which was never), I would make time for my family (which was never). I would email at all hours of the day and night and throughout the weekend, without the recognition I was essentially imposing the same rules on the entire organization (that we worked twenty-four hours a day, seven days per week). I was not yet in a position where I could talk compassion and suffering, because I had been taught the leadership theory of competence. I grew up in a world of competence. I had something to prove, and the world revolved around success, not significance.

This may be true for you too, and embracing your suffering may be part of your transition to compassionate leadership. Succeeding as a leader (subjective as this is), shouldn't mean failure as a person.

Evolving Toward a Life/Work Balance

It seems like such an obvious thing now, my realization that work/life just will not work because we create our own suffering through our lens of work as primary. I needed to move from a work/life orientation to a life/work balance.

But my story doesn't end there. Embracing a life/work balance was easy in principle—and nearly impossible in practice. It took daily reminders to put relationships first. I know firsthand how easy it is to arrive at work and fall right back into the world of competence.

If you do this, you are suffering, but mostly with yourself. Perhaps this first step toward compassionate leadership is critical for self-awareness ... but mostly you will suffer alone. And you may have suffered, and suffered, and suffered like this for years.

If you are trying to achieve a work/life balance, maybe you try to make up time on evenings and weekends, but it's mostly to no avail. When you really let go of your own critical self-analysis in this area, you can become a more fully compassionate leader. By letting go of your own lens and self-judgments and seeking to connect more deeply through sharing your suffering with others, you will finally begin to make progress.

For me, this includes sharing with the people I am closest to on the leadership team. By opening up, you essentially give permission for them to open up to you—and when the floodgates open, they really open. You will discover most people are suffering many of the same feelings as you but didn't feel comfortable saying anything for fear they would be seen as weak (back to strong/weak, fragile, competent).

Your conversations will evolve to life/work over work/life. This is the moment when you commit to never sending a before- or after-hours email or text message about work again. I made it a point to start conversations with something personal about myself and encourage others to do the same. This is vulnerability at the highest level.

Early on in these conversations, we are establishing trust. When we share personal information with others, there is always the possibility they will use that information to hurt us. "Did you hear the boss earlier? His life is in shambles." If they share that information with other employees, they are essentially creating a power base. They have personal, private information about me they are willing to share with others.

In the world of power theory (and there are mountains

of books on this topic), one person uses information to gain power over another. As a leadership teams, we must be explicit about the power structures most organizations have in place that would erode our confidence in and compassion for each other. You must make a conscious effort to resist that pull. Put simply, you must desire to be better than most.

In time, you find that you move away from trust and towards unconditional faith in each other. There is an unbreakable (anti-fragile) togetherness when you know you could share your lives with each other and always be compassionate with one another.

Most importantly to establishing unconditional faith is the realization that you would never create your own suffering through judgement (self-imposed or outside). Remember where we started this chapter, with your strong emotions about something and the discord between how you think it should be and the way it is, which creates your suffering. Accept things for how they are (withhold judgement) and find unconditional faith.

Setting Real-Life Priorities

This is where we encourage you to think about individuals in your personal life, whether it is your spouse, your children, your parents, or other loved ones. Have you put them first? Do they have unconditional faith in you and know you would drop everything for them? Are you guilty of being around them but also working?

Make no mistake, "I don't have time" is code language for "I don't care." We make time for the things we care about. We promised at the beginning of this book to take you through more and more difficult conversations as you get deeper into compassionate leadership. Early in our careers, neither Sarah nor I were ready for this type of conversation. We both lacked the emotional maturity and wisdom to realize a life of success is not the same as a life of significance. Now we know better. As the great Maya Angelou said, "I did then what I knew how to do. Now that I know better, I do better."

Your life is all about the path and not the destination. Today is a great day to make a new promise to yourself, your family, and your team. If you put life before work, you will send a message more powerful than words. You will send a message that will cross boundaries, change lives, and impact the future.

It will be hard, and you will be judged by others who will want to impose their view, label, and value judgement on you. The best thing you can do for them is to embrace, without accepting, their suffering. Help them understand the reason for their value label, that they have a privileged view of reality, and that their suffering is because of their judgement. It doesn't make them right or wrong, it only makes them suffer. Compassionate leadership is to "suffer with," not "suffer for."

Creating a Culture of Belonging

The next time you sit down for a meeting with more than four people at work, ask yourself how many people in the meeting are fitting in. Pay attention to dress, hair, and makeup, to the language used, to who set the meeting agenda, to when people showed up, and other details. Make a note of them.

We hear a lot about the Millennial workforce and how disrespectful they are—and we think this is utter nonsense. We think there has been a growing push in the last two or three decades away from "fitting in." Traditionally, we have relied on power structures, a sense of corporate culture, and institutional history to ensure people "fit in" to our culture. The problem with fitting in is that it is one sided. The interview process is designed to make sure the hiring side finds someone who "fits" and the person being hired is looking for a "match." Somewhere between "match" and "fit" is the perfect employee.

Our initial thinking was that organizations need to find ways to better engage employees. This happens in three spheres. 1) Do the employees have an intellectual connection to the work and organization, and are they being challenged appropriately? 2) Do they have an organizational connection to the company's spirit? 3) Do they have a social connection within the workspace?

We still believe this three-part theory is true. Improve any one of these three areas, and employee engagement and retention will improve. We have yet to find a case where this doesn't apply. We learned this from watching countless students go off to college. Every year, some would thrive and others would fail. The realization dawned that the secret to successful engagement for the student is the three questions above. Students who stayed grounded to high school friends and didn't make new college friends often failed. Students who weren't challenged intellectually failed. Those who didn't connect to the college socially organization failed—and at a much higher rate.

It turns out this theory for college engagement works at the organizational level as well. Call it a theory of better organizational engagement. Take this idea and make it work for you.

Finally, we want to get back to "match" and "fit." Since we can't really control the match side of the equation because this is the employee's perspective, we will focus on fitting in. An organization that focuses on fitting in also focuses on a judgement about the employee and their fitness to the organization. It feels like a judgement because it is.

As stated previously, our beliefs become our procedures, our policies, and ultimately, our culture. Your hiring policies are built on judgement criteria. One of the first messages you send to a potential new employee is a covert message: "You will be judged here." Is this really the best way to ensure you are hiring the best employees? We seriously doubt it.

A fragile way to hire is to look at fit. Someone may be strong or weak, but your organization is fragile in thought because if everyone fits in, you run a severe risk of groupthink. Prioritizing fitting in over good ideas is a recipe for disaster. If you want to build a corporate culture that is antifragile, you must walk away from policies, procedures, practices, and a covert culture that emphasize fitting in.

The antifragile approach to fitting in is a sense of belonging. We want employees to bring themselves to work. We want their personalities, their insecurities, their "best selves," their creative brains, and everything else—the good, the bad, and the ugly.

Any responsible HR manager is reading this right now and saying, "But if they belong, they may not comply with xxx procedure or policy." The first thing that comes to mind here is the dress code. To which, we respond, "Great." Your suffering around the dress code is because of a self-imposed value judgement.

We'll use a very specific example to help flesh out this point. If you believe it is important to wear a coat and tie to work every day, you must first back away from this notion to recognize you have a value label connected to coats and ties. The first question is whether this value judgement is warranted. It might be total nonsense, in which case the conversation should end there. If, however, we can make a reasonable case for why a coat and tie are appropriate—such as the maxim that "how you dress is how you are perceived and how you are perceived is how you are treated" (which happens to be what we actually believe)—then you can share your suffering with the people you hire.

You can start a conversation by saying, "I want you to belong here, and I believe the work we do matters in the lives of others. I have noticed we are not perceived or treated as professionals in some environments, and we are working against ourselves at those times." Being open to others' suffering, you can take a more balanced approach to dress code, and instead of a "policy," you can have a conversation. We can show competence when necessary and be compassionate along the way.

Setting new values is important in establishing organizational change. When a new value leads to behaviors that result in desired outcomes, the result is that those values and behaviors become embedded in the cultural DNA of the organization.

TRANSFORMATIONAL LEADERSHIP IN PRACTICE

BREE LANGEMO

Director of Entrepreneurship and Assistant Professor of Law and Entrepreneurship, Concordia College

One of the preeminent entrepreneurial thinkers in higher education lives and works in an unlikely place: a metro area of 246,000 residents just a couple of hours south of the Canadian border. Lawyer and educator Bree Langemo exemplifies the definition of entrepreneurship as the self-directed pursuit of opportunities to create value for others—whatever the field, wherever the location.

Bree directs the Entrepreneurship Center at Concordia College's Offutt School of Business in Moorhead, Minnesota. It's a small, private liberal arts college just across the river from her hometown of Fargo, North Dakota, and just down the road from her alma mater, the University of Minnesota-Moorhead.

Throughout her career in entrepreneurship, Bree has come to believe that vulnerability is the key to human connection. This was especially true during the two years as she navigated her role as a professor, providing support to her students for the stress and mental health challenges brought about by the COVID pandemic. "I try to be as authentic and honest as I can be, especially with my students," she said. "I tell them I'm a human first and a professor second, and if you need someone to talk to—it doesn't just have to be about academics—I'm always here."

Amid all the challenges brough about by the pandemic, Bree saw a silver lining in the compassion that people extended. She noticed this being lifted up over and over in her students' course evaluations. "Knowing that students saw I cared is the number one thing I would like to see continue as we emerge from the pandemic," she said. "We can all be more successful when we know people care. It's when we think people don't care, or we're not valued, or we're not seen, that we start to disengage."

Making a Living and Making a Life

Midway through the pandemic, Bree's college launched a symposium that grappled with the questions of what is work and what is the future of work? Throughout the symposium, speakers and audiences explored all aspects of work, including one theory that maybe work won't exist in the future if you followed the theory of the leisure economy. And if that were the case, what might humans do if work weren't a part of their lives and their identities? Would people be okay if they didn't work, considering we tie so much of our identity to work?

The discussion unveiled an entire range of uncertainty that many people experienced as COVID disrupted their work. "For some time now, I've been thinking a lot about work—meaningful work," Bree said, "and I think work is play and play is work and that's the way it should feel. And if it feels like work, as we've traditionally defined it, that's not really the kind of work I want to do anymore. And that's one thing that drew me to entrepreneurship. When we can align our own interests, skills, and abilities with the needs of others and create value for others, we find more meaning in what we're doing because we're pursuing purposeful work."

Throughout the symposium, they discussed automation and the advancement of technology through an optimistic lens, including how to eliminate some of the tasks that humans don't get a lot of meaning out of, and creating more work that's based on human skills such as compassion.

For example, Bree said, "You can't replace a nurse who has bedside manner to help a patient and express empathy. We encouraged students to start thinking about vocation—and not vocation in the technical sense but finding purpose and determining how to seek out a job with purpose, which is a big concept for students when they're eighteen or nineteen years old."

Pay Attention to the Flow

Viktor Frankl, who wrote the book *Man's Search for Meaning* after surviving a Nazi concentration camp, was skeptical about people who were lost in the search for purpose. He found they tended to report more dissatisfaction with life than people who accepted the journey of finding meaning in work, love, and the ability to rise above oneself—even (or perhaps especially) when that journey included suffering.

This leads to the possibility that many of us may initially have only minimal interest in the task(s) we're pursuing, but eventually those minor interests could turn into more. That's when Bree encourages us to take notice. "If you stick with something, you might get a little interest, and it's when you start getting more and more engaged in a topic that you should really pay attention—when you start to fall into flow. If you do fall into flow in a certain activity, it's worth mastering those skills. But don't just master them; do them so well that people will pay you for them. Paying attention to that flow state and your level of engagement is the key. It's about focusing on the journey and not getting hung up on the search."

Prioritizing Usefulness to Others

When Bree was the dean of business at a college in Colorado

Springs, she never thought she would leave education. But she became so compelled by the entrepreneurial mindset and the core of that idea, how to be most useful to others, that she went on to become the president of the Entrepreneurial Learning Initiative. The concept was so meaningful to her that it made her think more about her life and the value she wanted to create.

Bree believes part of our journey starts with being more useful beyond just our work. This can be in how we volunteer or provide to our community or serve our friends and family. "I didn't make that decision [to leave academia] without intention. I most definitely paid attention to what I'm good at and where I wanted to pursue more mastery," she reflected. "Understanding the entrepreneurial mindset became fascinating to me and my own career journey. For example, my current role is a new position that I helped shape. I knew what I wanted to do with this work, and I got the opportunity to help create it. I would never have had that level of determination and intention 10 years ago, but I've paid attention to what I'm good at and where I can create the most value."

Being Vulnerable—Even When It's Hard

Bree has noticed that when we pay attention to our emotions when we are feeling frustrated, often our natural instinct is to react in anger, but she always asks herself (and those around her) the same question: How can I be vulnerable in this moment to achieve a better outcome?

"It's more difficult to be willing to be vulnerable and actually share the deep emotion that we felt and experienced, but it is actually way more effective," she said. "I've even had supervisors with whom I've used this approach, and they've said, 'Whoa, I thought I was coming into a battle, but you disarmed me immediately.'"

Vulnerability can most definitely be disarming, but its effectiveness isn't limited to challenging situations, frustrations, or conflicts. There are other ways we can practice vulnerability. "I encourage my students, family, and colleagues to be willing to open themselves up more to people," Bree said. "We often still think of work and personal life as black and white. That's not where job satisfaction or great teams come from. There's a blending and understanding of the whole person when we're in work together with people that requires us to share and be vulnerable."

But to be clear, Bree doesn't think we should try to be everything to everyone. This discernment requires practice. "Know your audience. Part of this is about knowing when it's appropriate to share and being mindful of the overshare. There's a certain level of vulnerability you might have with a roomful of 300 people versus your executive team. Some people are really good at knowing when and how to be vulnerable, and others have to practice it. But anybody can practice something and master it if they find it to be worthy of mastering."

Building Strength Through Vulnerability

It may seem counterintuitive that being vulnerable with our staff and our teams can strengthen our relationships, but Bree believes this is absolutely the case. "I don't think you can ever really get to know another person unless you're willing to be vulnerable in that connection and in that relationship," she said. "Even with my students, I want them to know me beyond just being the professor in the classroom, and I want them to know some relatable experiences that I've had. It's not all about me, but it's about them building trust and rapport with me."

She believes that creates an atmosphere in the room and in the relationship that opens the door to a student showing up later and saying, "Hey, you know, I'm really struggling with something, could you help me?" Bree believes that happens because they were able to build a stronger connection, and ultimately because she used vulnerability to build connection in the relationship with that student.

Bree shared her belief that when people think about vulnerability, they often equate it with weakness. She thinks that's unfortunate—and definitely not accurate. "If we are not willing to be vulnerable, we will never create that authentic relationship with another human," she explained. "Throughout the many environments I've worked, if I haven't felt psychologically safe to speak up, I know there's something a little off. That means the environment doesn't make me feel good, ... and ultimately that doesn't make me feel effective or engaged in what I do. That's when I start looking for other work."

It may have been a factor that contributed to The Great Resignation of 2021, when people started leaving their employers at higher rates than ever before, even at the risk of financial instability. "They were redefining what work is to them," Bree said. "Whenever we see human behavior that relates to work, and we should start paying attention and fostering this idea of vulnerability and connection—because in the end, that's really all we've got."

CHAPTER 6

FROM COMPLICATED TO COMPLEX

This brings us to a pivotal evolution in your leadership. Regardless of your position or industry, we live in a world that has changed and evolved. Much of what we have been laying out over the course of this book is the need for our leadership language to shift. What is fundamentally driving this shift, though? This is a guiding question that frames and re-frames our work.

In this chapter, we move from a more theoretical need for change towards a more practical recognition that this train has already left the station. The leaders who embrace the new language are already "on the train," and those who haven't are getting the final wave of the hand to jump on board.

Where We Started

Everything used to be complicated. Whatever your leadership position or title, I can promise you that several decades ago, your work was very complicated. It required expertise to do well. It required training. It required a certain level of experience. That's because the complicated work of leadership is as much conceptual as it is practical. In order to make a decision, one needed to take in information. This was pre-internet, so no googling. To take information in, a leader needed to talk with people. They needed access. Usually this included many different groups. Leaders were capturing insights and knowledge and storing it all in their heads. But they also relied on experience. They knew stuff, and this made them experts. They had to be smart. They had to have answers.

Everything you just read was true before the advent and acceptance of the internet. (Also note a few things about what you just read. First, virtually everything about how we defined leadership was competence-based, with judgement being the only way to talk about effectiveness. The leadership language of competence worked in this framework because there was no other way to lead! Second, how many leadership books still basically revolve around this leadership framework? Sadly, the answer is most. Some leadership has begun to honor the reality that leadership is changing, but very few have mapped out a framework for how, why, and what we should be doing differently.)

In your leadership evolution, one of the most important things we hope you will glean from this book is that there are only two types of decisions that come to your desk as a leader. They are either complicated or complex—and how you handle each is dramatically different.

Two Types of Decisions

Complicated problems have one right answer. They require expertise and experience and all the other things leaders accumulated in the past. Complicated problems continue to exist in all of our organizations. They reinforce those things in our organizations that make us fragile, such as profit margins and achievement outcomes.

Complex problems, on the other hand, never have one right answer. With complex problems, there is no such thing as privileged information. Different experiences lead people to believe different things. For example, we recently lived through a global pandemic. If I had asked you, "What is the best way to keep kids and teachers safe from COVID?" you would have had an answer. And you might have bristled if another leader assumed they knew better or knew more than you. With some focused search and research time on a high-speed internet connection, you could have easily eclipsed my knowledge about what schools around the country did or what medical professionals advised or what lit up parent groups on Facebook. There was no way one person could amass all the information and deliver "the answer." Complexity is inherently unknowable.

The leader's job is to sort the complicated from the complex. The work of the organization is to answer the complicated questions. There is a staff for the complicated. The staff will be held accountable, and there should be an accountability system in place that allows for external stakeholders to understand the benefit of the organization. The language we use in this space is (mostly) competence based.

It should dawn on you that as problems or questions work their way through the organization, that the organizational chart serves a slightly different purpose. Effective (medium or large) organizations are structured in such a way that complicated questions and problems are filtered as they work up through the organization. As problems work through the organizational chart, what hits the desk of the CEO should be what remains: the complex.

To reinforce the need for language change, picture a CEO who has a staff solving the complicated and passing along the complex. Should this CEO then treat these complex problems as complicated? The stakeholders simply would not buy it. They would ask, "What makes this person think they have some privileged view of reality?" Their perspective would be that the CEO was demanding their obedience and requiring them to subordinate their will because the leader somehow know more than the rest.

This happens every single day in the sphere of public leadership, from schools and municipalities to county, state, and federal governments. The private sphere is slightly different—and a point I will come back to—but let us start with the public sphere because it is so much easier to see when it is going well, and even more plain to see when done poorly.

Complexity in the Public Sphere

When a public sphere leader stands in front of a group and indicates they have worked with "experts" behind closed doors to come up with a plan, do you buy it? I don't.

There is no one right way to make decisions when it comes to local, state, and federal taxes. These are all of great public concern, and people intuitively understand there are many different options at any given time. When the leader trots out "the" solution, they then face an insurmountable task of selling the solution. I don't want to be sold. This is why we despise the word "buy-in." People rarely buy into something they didn't help create.

Let us get very granular here at a precise moment when most local tax decisions occur (school, municipal, or county). There is an important distinction between questions like "Should we enact a tax rate increase?" and "How do we enact a tax rate increase?" The process for how to levy taxes is very complicated and requires many experts. We can (and should) hold ourselves accountable for the complicated parts of levying taxes. Competence-based language is okay here and should be encouraged.

But to treat both questions as complicated is a recipe for failure. The first question, "Should we enact a tax rate increase?" has many related components such as when, how much, etc. In the public sphere, the best way to ensure all citizens feel fully informed to make an individual decision about taxes is complex—and, as such, it requires compassionate language.

Compassion is about suffering. For our leaders to demonstrate that they share our suffering, they might say, "Having our citizenry fully informed about our future in this community and what that means for our taxes requires us to have a conversation. I want for [not want from] us to feel comfortable with our collective decision. I want for us to be able to open up fully, and I am suffering with how best to do that."

This response would have asked our citizens to share their suffering. People would have been provided with an opportunity to say vulnerable things like, "My family is under financial strain, and additional taxes will mean I must cut other areas of spending. I am worried about the impact on home values. I am worried about the timing."

When leaders do not embrace the complex with compassion, what happens? Many take to social media, where we feel we are heard. This, of course, does not really happen since we mostly create echo chambers (because of who we choose to follow and unfollow), so our suffering becomes compounded, and we are not fully exposed to the suffering of others. Instead, we too often judge others for their suffering.

The net effect of all of this is a massively missed opportunity. Instead of constructive depolarization, we end up with the opposite, a fully polarized division. It becomes a matter of who is right and who is wrong. We reinforce competence and the complicated in addressing a problem that was inherently complex and required compassion. Our language perpetuated the problem.

Pay special attention if you are leading in the public sphere, because much of our work with the public is complex, and a complicated mindset is our undoing.

As we embrace the complex for what it is, our brains should begin doing backflips. How could you possibly involve everyone in every decision? This creates a cognitive dissonance for us because many of our organizational structures are built around the complicated. We have to create the systemic architecture that allows space for us to bring complex issues to our respective communities.

Let's start with a small scale and work our way up. In a community of 1,000 or less, it is not impossible to get a representative group together to solicit the voices of the community. How does the focus group feel about this decision? Send the focus group out to get input and bring that back (being aware of bias, of course). You could essentially make space for every voice to be heard if they want to participate. Not easy, but possible.

The leader of this small community who is tasked with a complex problem should not go to the residents with the solution worked out and then try to sell it. Instead, the leader should go to the community first with vulnerability, without an answer but with a really good question. They should share their own suffering, ask others to share their suffering, and then pose the question. (Posing the right question is an art in itself. For a primer on how to do that, I highly recommend *Scaling Conversations: How Leaders Access the Full Potential of People* by Dave MacLeod.)

When compassionate suffering is connected and responses are drawn together, residents get to share their expertise and learn the thoughts of others. When a consensus is reached, a community is depolarized.

With larger communities, this approach becomes much more difficult in person. This is when we become reliant on technology to help. Many companies offer different strategies for crowdsourcing information, but the essential approach is similar: By allowing users to share their insights, then sharing how others have responded, the programs make users aware of other perspectives. This approach tends to move users to being more open and learning, even if they were initially closed and knowing. This is the single biggest paradigm shift our public makes as it relates to complex issues.

It bears repeating here that the public sphere leader who creates a solution by treating a complex problem as if it were complicated, and then takes it to the community for buy-in, is in effect saying the community inherently does not know what to do and they should leave it to the smart people in leadership to figure it out. Surveys are a classic example of how to do this. You have a solution, and you ask people to essentially vote on it before you reveal the answer and let everyone know whether they guessed correctly or not.

Further, the notion of being the smartest person in the room has changed. "Smart" actually used to be a strategic advantage prior to the internet. Knowing stuff had value. If you compared yourself to others in the community, maybe you actually were the smartest in the room. Now, however, being smart can be a disadvantage in a complex world. If you think you have "the answer," you are not only wrong, but you will offend others in the process.

Being smart is not a sustainable competitive advantage in the globally networked world. Very quickly, your smartness becomes irrelevant. Instead, the ability to manage networked crowdsourcing around the complex is the sustainable advantage. You don't have to be the smartest in the room because you recognize the room itself is smarter than all of you individually.

The leader's job is to create the room and manage the space for the conversation. Empathy buries intelligence. This is why so many EQ books have been written recently. Many people recognize the need for this trait, but few have backed away enough to identify why. Empathy doesn't just make us feel good—it is essential to complex leadership.

Complexity in the Private Sphere

Do complex issues arise in private sphere leadership? Yes, all the time. It is much more nuanced than the public sphere, though. As an example, much of the work of product development is complicated and requires expertise. In many instances, you would never want to crowdsource these ideas, out of an abundance of caution to avoid releasing trade secrets to competitors.

What about the growth strategy, though ... is that complicated? Is there only one right answer? There are myriad ways to grow a company—and none is assured of success. Recently, I was on a call with a CEO of a small company when growth strategies came up in conversation. The CEO was striving to grow the user base and talking about what they might do. Minutes later, the CEO was talking about expanding the company's content offerings. These two strategies are fundamentally different ... more users or more content? Which is the better strategy?

This is where crowdsourcing could be tremendously insightful. Imagine if this CEO crowdsourced his employees to get insight to the question (note that we did not say to answer the question) and then crowdsourced the current customer base.

The formula is the same for public and private at this point. Start with compassion, and that means share the suffering. "As CEO, I need to finalize our growth strategy for the next quarter to build our base. I am wrestling with the question of whether we should expand content or acquire new users. What are some things we should consider when making this decision?" The ideas from this conversation will be far more insightful and useful than virtually anything the CEO comes up with on their own.

An important point here is that the CEO is not democratizing the company and asking people what to do. This would be a tactically dangerous approach because the question would never communicate the intent of the leader. Instead of asking "What should we do?" the leader asks "What things should we consider?" This is a nuanced point but one that is very important. (The purpose of this book is not to delve into the nuance of question style, but to understand the overarching construct. For a much deeper dive into great questions and question strategy, we again recommend *Scaling Conversations*.)

The leader who uses this approach now doesn't have to figure out how to get buy-in on the growth strategy. Buy-in is not needed when people feel invested in building the plan. "We helped make this decision" is a far more powerful motivator than "She made this decision for us." On top of that, when the CEO makes the decision and things don't work out, it's easy for virtually everyone to say, "I knew that wouldn't work."

The one place where public sphere and private sphere leadership directly overlap is the scale of the organization. Simply put, the larger the organization, the higher the likelihood the CEO is dealing in the world of complexity. Smaller organizations usually find the CEO also working in the realm of complicated. This is not a value statement of good or bad, just a function of size.

But Why? The Psychology of Decision-Making

We have been presenting on the difference between complicated and complex decision-making for many years, and during the presentations, we find people nodding their heads in agreement, almost universally agreeing with the concept. We have had the opportunity to counsel and mentor leaders and watch others who have heard the presentations and make a commitment to start using this framework as a guide when they get back to work and then ... go right back into old habits where everything becomes complicated.

Why is that? What is it about human psychology that makes us want to see the world as complicated? We have thought about this for years. We have talked with hundreds of leaders in both public and private spheres. While we may not have all the answers, we have some thoughts we would like to share with you.

Consider healthcare. Off the top of your head, you would think nearly all people would agree the medical field is complicated because it's filled with tasks that require special knowledge: how to give stitches, how to make a basic diagnosis, how to prescribe certain medications, and so on. Let's ponder cancer. There are many forms of cancer treatments. Doctors don't look at cancer as a complicated decision. They recognize there are many complicated strategies, and their job is to inform the patient, offer odds/success rates, and then make recommendations. Ultimately, it is the patient who must consent to a course of treatment.

That is where the complex meets the complicated. Doctors know where the complicated crosses over into the complex (unknowable), and they draw that line. The decision of how to live with cancer is different for each patient. Some are willing to go through excruciatingly small odds and great discomfort, and others are not. Neither is right, and neither is wrong. A complex decision is just like that, and this is why we spent so much time at the beginning of this book talking about language of competence/judgement and language of compassion. The cancer thing requires compassion—trust us.

Financial planning is rich with complicated pieces: the differences between Roth and traditional IRAs, equity investments, stock investments, stocks that pay dividends (or not), exchange traded funds, bonds, mutual funds, retirement schedules, pension distributions, and more. This short list doesn't even begin to scratch the surface of the complicated aspects of financial planning. So it would be easy to assume it is a complicated task. After all, the first thing consumers do when they get serious about financial planning is hire an expert.

Here's the thing, though. There is one major complex decision to be made: What is the best strategy for you? You don't know what the markets are going to do over time. You don't know when the next recession will hit. You may want to retire early. Great, but that doesn't help unless the advisor knows how you define retirement. It doesn't help if they don't know what standard of living you plan to maintain, or if you plan to travel. You may feel you need "more than enough," and yet, how you define enough varies from person to person.

This is why the financial planner always asks you about your goals and your risk tolerance. They try to ascertain the unknowable complex ("What does retirement mean for you?") so they can make informed and complicated recommendations. Ultimately, you are the one who decides what financial strategy you will choose among the myriad of complicated options.

These are just two examples to help set the stage for asking the question about why we want things to be complicated and not complex. Complicated has just one answer, and, with expertise, we can solve the formula to come up with the solution. We want cancer to be like the treatments, complicated and solvable. We cannot possibly predict how the financial markets will change over time, so we crave for it to be complicated. "Just tell me what I have to do to make it work out in the end."

Unfortunately, that is just not possible. If we are being blunt about the whole thing, the two biggest things we are trying to overcome are luck and risk. To understand this in a very deep way as it relates to money, I encourage you to read *The Psychology of Money: Timeless Lessons on Wealth, Greed, and Happiness* by Morgan Housel. Residual risk is what remains when you get to the point where you know everything that you think you need to know. Good luck and good fortune happen to all of us. You cannot possibly know how your body will react to treatment, and what works on one person may not be as effective on another. The luck of your genetics is part of the equation, and it's part of what makes something complex (unknowable).

Applied to us as leaders, this is a very simple point. We want everything to be complicated because we want to believe we are in control. Just like financial planning, and just like cancer.

But if we are honest, luck and risk are a big part of our lives. We don't know what our competitors are doing. We don't know if our product will come to market at just the right time or slightly miss the mark. The sheer volume of things we do not and cannot know is incredibly frightening for us, and we want to create some control. We do that by believing we can find the answer, and the only way to do that is to treat everything as complicated.

Embracing the truly complex means embracing the role of luck and risk in outcomes. If we perceive a problem to only be complicated, we will be blind to those variables. Put simply, we will miss the options available to us. Living only in a world of complicated forces to also live in a world of only right and wrong. We may be right from time to time, but eventually, we will be wrong. And although there are many ways things can go right, when things go wrong, we generally don't get a second chance. Giving ourselves the most options for success by seeing the world as complex is the long-term strategy for future success.

TRANSFORMATIONAL LEADERSHIP IN PRACTICE

JEFF PATTERSON

CEO, Gaggle

Jeff Patterson has always been curious. His family tells the storyy about how they knew right away that Jeff was an entrepreneur—and this continued throughout his childhood, from around age 4 into his high school years. "I've always had big plans to make a difference through the companies I created," he said. "But right after college, I did what I thought I was supposed to do, and I got a coveted job as an investment banker. But that only lasted one year. I just knew it wasn't for me."

While Jeff was working as an investment banker, he met a friend who had similar entrepreneurial motivations, and they started brainstorming business ideas.

"As soon as my bonus check cleared that first year, I quit my job to focus on our shared vision," Jeff recounted. "We had been staying up late every night after working investment banking hours and weekends to build our company. But that first company ended up being a terrible idea. It turns out that fax machines were not the future."

After that business, Jeff and his partner started an educational software program. "We didn't know anything about educational software, but we wanted to get involved. It was not a great business either, but we learned so much. And then I started making some more educational software, and I landed on the idea for Gaggle. I tried to raise venture capital back then, but no one trusted me, and I'm so glad that they didn't. I was stubborn and naïve, and I started bootstrapping it, and now we're at 150 employees. We don't have any outside investors, and I don't have an exit plan. I just want to do what's right for the world and for my staff."

The Key to Jeff's Success: Listening

"I have big ears. I listen for problems and challenges," Jeff said. "When I was at a conference years ago, I asked an educator about emailing with students, and she said, 'Oh, no, my district would never let our students have an email address.' I asked her why not, and she said safety and security were the primary issues. The naïve part of me decided right then to create a safe solution, and so we started a safe email program for students. Our tagline was "Hotmail where the teachers are in control."

From there, Jeff and his team kept refining and evolving the product along the way. Clients continued to ask for things like message boards and file storage, and what they created became almost a full LMS where safety and security was the secret sauce. "And then slowly, we realized the world didn't love our LMS; they just loved our safety. And the funding source that we were pursuing at the time changed, so we ended up pivoting away from that original product into safety. Ironically, we had already started the pivot, but I was just slow to the party. The world had already pushed us to that place."

It's Easy to Be a Peace-Time General

Pivoting away from the LMS and ultimately focusing solely on safety was a difficult decision for Jeff and the company. "When we were selling our LMS, Gaggle was up to $12 or $13 million in revenue—but when that program went away, we went backwards $3 million in revenue. I was self-funded, and I had bought out my partner not long before, so it was an incredibly stressful time," he recalled. "We had two rounds of layoffs, and there were days that it felt like the whole world was caving in on me and things seemed out of control. The sad thing is, I had already corrected the ship, but I was so close to it that I couldn't see that we were already in better waters."

Jeff believes that we all have unanswerable questions in us, things we're always striving to solve. For him, a key question continues to be *Am I doing the right thing?* "I know I want to be doing the right thing for my staff, and treating them with respect and compassion is a big part of that," he explained.

This also aligns with how Jeff feels about performance improvement plans and addressing challenges with employees who are not meeting expectations. "I hate performance improvement plans. They're demeaning; if things are not working out with an employee, I want to have those honest conversations, ideally very early. When it gets to that point, I'm going to say, 'Look, I'm willing to try to make this work, but you are great the way you are, and the changes I need may not be changes you want to make—and you don't need to change unless you want to.' If things aren't going to work out, I would rather just be more generous on severance. Even when we let people go, they have to leave with their dignity."

Create Space for Authentic Communication and Mistakes

Jeff admits that he loves making mistakes. "I love screwing up and getting to apologize. I think there's so much power in saying, "I'm sorry. I was wrong." He follows the advice of Chriss Voss, a former FBI lead hostage negotiator, in what he calls tactical empathy. He recommends having regular accusation audits, which for Jeff can sound like this: "'You're probably thinking I'm a jerk, or maybe you think I don't understand the issue.' I say all those things the other person might be thinking so it clears the space for us to have an honest conversation."

Jeff has found this practice is a humbling way to have more candid conversations with his peers, colleagues, and team members. "When you're leading a team, you need your people to be honest and vulnerable with you, but to do that, they need to feel safe. You don't want them to hide their problems and hide their own weaknesses. I'd rather that we identify our weaknesses and then work together to collaborate on a solution. Calling out our own shortcomings and our perceptions of others can create the space to have more impactful conversations."

Jeff admits that although he loves making mistakes, many of his team members don't particularly like mistakes because they want to be perfect right out of the gate. "My job is to push us into places that are uncomfortable, where we don't yet have all the answers, but I'm confident that we will find a solution."

He knows that because he's pushing his organization to do things they don't know how they're going to accomplish, they may at times resent him. He also acknowledged that both technical and human errors are going to happen. When there is a mistake, the team conducts a blameless retrospective, which is essentially an after-action report where they talk through what happened, what could have been done differently, and how the process can be corrected so that the incident does not happen in the future. The team also makes sure it has the necessary resources and tools to succeed moving forward.

Jeff related this to a character from *War and Peace*, in a scene where the Russian army is attacking France. They are getting routed. Things are beginning to collapse. But in one artillery battery in the center, Captain Tushin held his ground and kept firing.

His efforts led to the whole Russian army being able to execute a proper withdrawal.

"People celebrated how great they were to have achieved this withdrawal, not realizing there was this unknown captain who was the one who really made it all happen. This story reminds me that there are many Captain Tushins within my organization, and I need to make sure that they are honored and appreciated," he said.

Jeff keeps all of this in mind when he welcomes new members to the Gaggle team. "When a new employee starts, I call them and thank them for joining us, and I get to know a little bit more about them. The goal is to help them feel like they can communicate directly with me if they see something wrong or if they have concerns or questions."

Jeff also calls every single Gaggle employee on their work anniversary—and he admits this is definitely becoming more challenging as the company continues to grow. "Even though it's getting harder, I want to keep doing this because they're all Captain Tushins, and I need them to know that I care about them."

Know What You're Asking Your People to Do (and What's Too Much)

Jeff acknowledges that at Gaggle, they are indeed putting a lot of pressure on themselves to protect children and keep them safe, and that's more than some of their employees can handle. "I've had people who have left because they felt it was too much pressure. There's always something more that we could do, and more kids we should be protecting. I have to put that in perspective of what's maybe not even possible."

Jeff likens this to the battle of Cowpens in South Carolina during the Revolutionary War, a turning point which eventually led to a Patriot victory at Yorktown. The British Army was led by Banastre Tarleton, and Brigadier General Daniel Morgan commanded a small group of Continental soldiers and local militia. The night before the battle, General Morgan went to each of the militia campfires, and he said, "Boys, I know you're not soldiers. You're farmers. All I want you to do is stand your ground, and fire two volleys, and then you can drop your gun and run home. That's all I need you to do."

The next day on the battlefield, there was a small rise on the hill where General Morgan had posted the militia. As the British started coming in, they fired one volley. Most of them ran home after the first volley. Some of them fired a second, and then they too ran home. This led the British to think it was a rout, so they moved up over the hill—right into the Continental soldiers, who were holding their ground. The Continental army succeeded that day, losing only 72 men, compared to the more than 600 men lost by the British.

"The leadership message of that battle for me is not to ask more of my people than they're capable of doing," Dave said. "I recognize that we have some people who are great, but they're not going to be able to do maybe two other things—so instead of making their lives miserable or focusing on what they can't do, we celebrate what they can do. I want people to be happy, to feel safe, and for their job to have meaning and purpose so they can be proud of who they are and what they've accomplished."

Embracing Criticism with Compassion and Vulnerability

Recently Gaggle has come under fire for a variety of reasons, including what some lawmakers have called "a clear invasion of student privacy, particularly when students and families are unable to opt out." Critics have also expressed concerns about implicit bias, how the company handles LGBTQ+ students, and the validity of the company's safety benefits for school districts.

"We received a letter from U.S. Senator Elizabeth Warren that was the culmination of this criticism and what we're trying to do is protect students," Dave said. "The Senator's letter seemed to question whether there was proof that Gaggle makes a difference in saving students' lives. There's no denying that it's hurtful to hear this feedback when we are doing everything we can to protect our kids—to have people undermining us with accusations and claims. In fact, this criticism led school districts to delay their planned Gaggle implementations—and it's leaving students and educators vulnerable to suicide, harassment, pedophilia, and school shootings."

Despite these frustrations, the criticism has led Jeff and the Gaggle team to consider how they can improve and better support schools and districts. "We now have a new leader for machine learning algorithms whose priority is to ensure there is not any implicit bias within our algorithms. We are engaging The Trevor Project to evaluate how are we handling LGBTQ+ issues."

Jeff's openness to learning and growth is an asset in receiving this feedback gracefully. "Yes, this criticism has been challenging, but I like to see these things as opportunities for us to be better and improve, and we are definitely rising to that challenge. I frequently repeat the message, 'Never waste a good crisis.' Ultimately, having humility and listening to our people, our communities, and our biggest critics, is what really makes us leaders—especially when it's hard."

CHAPTER 7

FROM HIERARCHIES TO NETWORKS, MANAGEMENT TO LEADERSHIP

Treating everything as complicated means you are smart ... and smart is not a long-term success strategy.

Are the structures of leadership history the best platforms for carrying our leadership forward into the future? We are making a compelling case that the answer is no. The U.S. Nobel laureate economist Herbert Simon was the first to write about bounded rationalism in his 1982 book *Models of Bounded Rationality*. Bounded rationalism as a concept says decision-makers (irrespective of their level of intelligence) have to work under three unavoidable constraints: 1) Only limited, often unreliable, information is available regarding possible alternatives and their consequences. 2) The human mind has only limited capacity to evaluate and process the information that is available. 3) Only a limited amount of time is available to decide.

As a result, individuals who intend to make rational (best) choices are bound to make satisficing choices in complex situations. They pursue the minimum satisfactory outcome rather than maximizing or optimizing. Note the key word complex. These limits (bounds) on rationality also make it nearly impossible to draw up contracts (solutions) that cover every contingency, necessitating reliance on rules of thumb.

I have been playing with this idea for several years, and I suspect bounded rationalism still exists for many people and organizations around the world. As an individual facing a complex decision, you can't know everything, you can't evaluate everything, and you don't have unlimited time, so you settle.

I have also come to believe that, as a society, we have a choice to unbind the concept of bounded rationalism when facing complex decisions. Specifically, we can unbind #1 and #2 above. If a leader should choose to involve one other person in a complex solution, they have potentially doubled the amount of information available and doubled their evaluative efforts (if they have some way of learning together). Involve four people in the effort and quadruple your "limited capacity" for information and evaluation. You can quickly discern that with additional people involved in the process, you can grow decision-making capacity exponentially.

Let's dig in a bit deeper into how we can involve others via crowdsourcing, which we introduced in a previous chapter. Crowdsourcing is not a new phenomenon. It was first employed by Francis Galton in 1906 at the West of England Fat Stock and Poultry Exhibition, when 787 people guessed the weight of a steer. Their average guess was 1,197 pounds. The actual weight of the steer was 1,198 pounds. This three-sentence story opens the door to the power of crowdsourcing. Studies have been conducted and replicated, and the results are almost always the same: The power of the crowd is almost always greater than any one individual. Even when the individual is an expert. Stock markets, political polls, and many other examples all give evidence there is something at work here.

Imagine crowdsourcing the number of jellybeans in a jar. Similar to the contest to guess the weight of a cow, just gather a bunch of people, take guesses, and then average the guesses. This average will likely be closer than any one of the individual guesses. If the guesses when averaged are so good, imagine the power of crowdsourcing major corporate or government decisions. Hold this concept in your mind as you think about how you might create an organizational chart to represent this? You obviously can't.

Organizational charts have been described in many ways, and one of the best we've ever heard is that organizational charts are simply a pyramid of garbage cans. The very nature of an organizational chart is such that the middle managers vet information. They create a series of filters. If a "problem" can be solved, it should be solved before it makes it to the desk of the CEO. If the CEO is on information overload, then the organizational chart is also suffering from filter failure.

There is an important bifurcation happening here that we have touched on several times throughout this book. This bifurcation is where complex and complicated part ways. Some problems have a solution that might require expertise to solve. Other problems are vague and maybe even unknowable (such as "When will the next hurricane hit the Gulf Coast?"). There are just these two types of problems, and this is an important concept. Some problems can be solved by the hierarchy. These problems have a solution. Some problems rise to the CEO level and don't have just one answer, but rather a myriad of ways of perceiving data and information and countless potential solutions. These are not problems for the hierarchy, but problems for the networks.

This is where management and leadership come into play. As author J.R. Woodward writes in *Creating a Missional Culture: Equipping the Church for the Sake of the World*, "[W]hile management acts within culture, leadership creates culture" (p. 20). There are countless books that describe the difference between management and leadership, but as we described leadership at the beginning of this book as building relationships from the middle to work on tough issues, so too, is the function of management.

Management is not "less than" or "greater than" leadership. Management makes leadership possible. Management solves problems. Management makes plans. Management moves the organization forward. Organizations cannot exist without competent management (pay special attention to the word competent, as we have discussed this in previous chapters too). Management requires competence because it solves problems. The problems it solves have one answer, and it's either right or wrong. Managers have specialties, expertise, and experience. One would never consider crowdsourcing management. Management serves a very specific and invaluable purpose.

Everyone in the organization is a manager, from the CEO to the custodian. We manage tasks and work. We now live in a society, however, that cannot support managing people. In today's world, if you have to be managed, you are unemployable. If you manage—and as a leader, you do—then you recognize the need for "smartness" in an area (or multiple areas).

Let's talk about smartness and long-term survival for a moment. Decades and decades ago, being smart was probably an advantage. If you could be the smartest person doing your job in a relatively small town, you were the best. And if people mostly stayed home, you were good. If you were super-smart, maybe you were the best in a big city. If you have a small group of people to compare against, you can theoretically be smarter than they are. It is a lot like being the fastest or the strongest.

If the comparison group is small and local, you can possibly be the best. Even that is a bit of a gamble, though.

With the advent of the internet, the entire world changed. Being the smartest in the room no longer mattered because you could be compared to anyone else on the planet doing similar work. Being smart didn't just become irrelevant, we believe it became a liability. The world has become amazingly complex and is rapidly changing. To say you are the smartest is to say you are on top of everything. That is absurd. Further, confirmation bias will lead you to believe you have answers when it is likely others have better answers. Being smart in a complex world might be slightly helpful in a moment, but over the long term, it is a recipe for disaster. Somebody somewhere will come up with something better at some point, and you would miss the opportunity to capitalize on their genius. And because of the global availability of information, anyone in your organization could look to this idea online and say, "Why didn't we do that? You weren't very smart, were you?"

In a globally connected and complex society, the ability to manage both social and information networks is the most essential element in a long-term success strategy. The real skills for long-term success are relationship building, empathy, humility, and compassion. Intelligence might account for 1% of a long-term success strategy, and the other 99% consists of power skills deployed across a social network.

The evolution from manager to leader is hard for everyone.

The manager uses a language and conceptual framework for the work that doesn't apply to the task of leadership. Countless books talk about moving from the dance floor to the balcony, or differentiating between customer complaints and owner concerns, or about the difference between management and leadership, but in reality, very few books talk about the conceptual framework and the language we use within these contexts.

Customer complaints are a management issue (with the appropriate hierarchy, framework, and accompanying language). Owner concerns are a leadership issue (with appropriate network frameworks and accompanying language). Far too many managers are not taught the true language of leadership, and, thus, they bring the language of management they have always spoken to their leadership role.

Think of a recent example of a problem you have framed as complicated when it may have been complex. How did you use the framework of hierarchy to solve it? What language did you use? What was the impact? How might you have used a network? What would have been the impact?

Finally, let us revisit management and leadership within the context of fragile and antifragile. Jim Collins, the author of *Good to Great: Why Some Companies Make the Leap and Others Don't*, speaks of a poignant distinction between being the "time-teller" and the "clock-builder."

Since we know most organizations are systemically built in such a way as to resist change, an inevitable collision is bound to occur when the organization doesn't want to change and looks to the "expert" leader to solve the problems. The expert/competent leader must resist this temptation, because accepting the paradigm means reinforcing competence culture. It becomes a competence doom loop.

This is especially perilous because of the fear of failure around change (fragile). Remember, people don't inherently fear failure, but they do fear blame. For a leader, failure could mean the loss of a job (survival), community (acceptance), or reputation (competence), to name just a few. We feel a draw towards security and stability that comes with being considered an expert, but this is a false hope because it remains fragile. You're only an expert until something goes wrong, then you become the fool.

Your organization will not change until you manifest a change in your leadership. Although this sounds blunt, we feel it is accurate to note that we either need new leaders who are ready to re-make the future or current leaders of every level who have the courage and creativity that has eluded them to date. "Conceptually stuck systems cannot become unstuck simply by trying harder. For a fundamental reorientation to occur, that spirit of adventure which optimizes serendipity and which enables new perceptions beyond the control of our thinking processes must happen first," writes Edwin Friedman, a rabbi and family therapist, in *A Failure of Nerve: Leadership in the Age of the Quick Fix* (p. 24).

TRANSFORMATIONAL LEADERSHIP IN PRACTICE

SHAILY BARANWAL

CEO and Founder, Elevate K-12

Shaily Baranwal is an extreme nonconformist. A first-generation immigrant to the United States, Shaily was born and raised in Mumbai, India, and she credits her enthusiasm for entrepreneurship to her desire to follow where her intrinsic passions lead.

"If the whole world moves in a certain direction, I have zero interest in going in that direction. It's just who I am," Shaily said. "I have always followed my passion. Money has never driven me. My father founded one of the leading research and development healthcare equipment companies in India, so I saw entrepreneurship happening in my family every single day of my life. Now he's 75, and he just started another company."

Shaily has always had a creative, analytical brain. She received an industrial production engineering degree in school, but she very quickly realized that was not what she wanted to do. "I went in search of finding my own path. I joined a band. I dabbled with theater. For me it was not about the money; it was about doing what I love to do and exploring where that could lead. I'm an introvert who grew up with many different special needs. I used to stammer. My whole childhood was about trying to figure myself out," she recalled.

"Eventually, all that exploration led me to get a teaching degree in India, followed by a few years' stint as a teacher." Shaily's family didn't understand her decision. "It was so different from the other very successful paths that they had taken," she said. "They pointed out how I was making a quarter of what I would have made as an engineer. The point is, money was not important; I just wanted to find something I loved, and I have stuck with that my entire career."

When Shaily realized that she wanted to make a bigger impact beyond classroom teaching, she pursued her MBA at the University of Michigan, where she received an entrepreneurial scholarship. "My real life actually started when I came to the U.S. and I conceptualized my company, Elevate K12, while I was in business school."

After receiving her MBA, Shaily worked as a management consultant in Chicago with AT Kearney. After a few years in consulting, she moved back to India and started a chain of preschools in rural India. She also launched the country's first live grill restaurant, which she sold in 2015 to India's largest food and beverage conglomerate, Dabur.

"As an entrepreneur, I simply want to find problems that I can solve through the companies I start," Shaily said. "My passion still comes from looking at my customers and seeing how happy they are using my products. I wish I could live inside the heart and brains of my customers to gauge their every reaction to the usage of our products and services."

But a personal loss in mid-2014 prompted Shaily to pack everything in India and move back to the United States. "I decided to go back to the idea that I had in business school, and I converted that into what became Elevate K-12," she said. "I raised my first round of funding from a Chicago-based hedge fund in 2016, and we haven't looked back since."

Elevate K-12 is one of the first large companies that evolved out of the University of Michigan's Entrepreneurial Center. Shaily now sits on its board to advise students on how to take their passions and convert those ideas into meaningful businesses.

"With Elevate K12, my goal was to disrupt the K-12 education industry with an entirely new category," she said. "My passion is to solve the world's biggest problems, and I saw that one of the biggest challenges facing school districts was the fast-growing teacher shortage. ... We are a live teaching company, where we take a classroom space and convert it into a live room where our teacher—who could be working from home in another state than where the school is—streams live into the classroom. We have built our own technology and designed the whole live teaching experience around it," Shaily explained. "We are truly creating a new category."

"When I started the company, people thought it sounded crazy. But that's because it was ahead of its time," she said. "That's why we prioritized gaining proof of concept from our early adopters before launching into the pragmatist phase and scaling fast to reach more students and classrooms."

Having Compassion for Ourselves First

Over time, Shaily's learning has extended to her role as a leader. "I made mistakes earlier in my career where I led people with a complete lack of compassion," she acknowledged. "I remember having a conversation with Quintin about this after I had lost a couple of people because I was not compassionate with them. He affirmed that I *could* become a compassionate leader."

That conversation with Quintin set Shaily on a learning journey. She began reaching out to other people and learning how they lead with compassion to help her understand how she could purposefully support her team. "As I really reflected, I realized I was avoiding difficult conversations," she said. "I knew if I were to have these difficult but necessary conversations, the person in front of me would be upset—but the avoidance of the conversations would create a chasm that would then burst, and it would damage the company."

Shaily attributes some of this to the high-growth nature of the organization. "Every six months, I have to reorganize and change processes because we are growing so quickly. If I'm not doing that, our company will not thrive the way I see it has the potential to. The demands are very different than my other two companies, which were not high-growth—which can make it more difficult to lead with compassion. Over time, I've learned how others approach this, and now I realize that I didn't really understand the definition of compassion, but what I've come to define it as for myself is being direct, open, and honest and always guiding our team through whatever decision is being made. It's not going to suit everyone, but by being transparent and clear about what's happening, it enables people to feel that they're a part of the process."

This is even more important when Shaily is in the process of deciding how the company is going to address a particular problem. She said she underestimated the amazing impact of showing vulnerability. By sharing with her team openly when she doesn't know the answer to something, she has given people within her organization an opportunity to be more open about their fears and create a free flow of risk-driven, innovative ideas. Her teams can now come up with their own ideas and create solutions that the leadership team may not have even considered.

"When COVID happened, we shared the fact that we didn't know what we were going to do. We have a team of 100 employees in India and 100 employees in the U.S., and we have over 1,000 teachers, so we are an organization of about 1,200 people. It can be difficult to make sure that you are communicating effectively with everyone," Shaily said. "To help address that, I joined weekly calls with two different groups because the message into each team was different. I shared that I had no idea what was going to happen, but I can tell you that we're going to assess the scenario every two weeks, and we are going to make the best decisions with the data points that we have right now."

It worked. "The moment I started doing that," Shaily recalled, "I began to see my leaders embrace the same direct and honest approach within their own teams."

Sharing Bad News Compassionately

As with any company, there are times when the leadership approach doesn't resonate with an individual. In these cases, Shaily believes it's important to have honest communication with the employee and provide opportunities for them to grow. "If there is resistance, or if the change isn't being seen to scale, then sometimes we need to make a decision to part ways, and to do so with compassion," she said. "But if people are open to learning how to best meet the needs of their role and convert that learning into action, these individuals will work out."

Because the company is growing so quickly, there have been many tough conversations about repurposing roles and scaling functions. "The first job of a leader is to find the right team members who have the right skills for each position—but even more importantly, they need to have the right mindset," Shaily said. "When they don't have the right mindset, I am direct, honest, and compassionate about how this is not the right environment for them."

In keeping with this approach, Elevate K-12 identifies key skill sets at the screening level of the interview process, which has helped it identify skilled, effective individuals whose mindsets align from the beginning.

Listen to Feedback, But Don't Create a Democracy

Shaily and her team regularly solicit feedback from others on the leadership team—and everyone throughout the organization—using periodic pulse surveys to gather quantitative and qualitative data points. "We have an open forum where we share back with the team what we've heard, how we're going to address their input, and what people are excited about," she said. "We call these 'Ask Shaily Anything!'"

Teaching her teams the power of decision-making so that the organization as a whole has a system behind it is very important to Shaily. She recommends asking three questions every time there is a decision that needs to be made: 1) Is it an emergency so much that it must be decided on immediately? 2) What are the key, qualitative gut measures that can inform the decision? 3) Is there a timeline for achieving the answer?

"There is never just one right answer when you're making a decision," Shaily said. "There are always multiple ways to look at the problem. You might decide to go with one route because of your experiences and pattern recognition for that kind of decision-making, but there are always two answers or multiple paths to achieving success."

Shaily has approached her life decisions with a similar candor—always following her passion. "Nothing fazes me. I am like an Energizer bunny," she joked. "Success or failure, I will always stop and check and learn from each and keep on moving. Life is all about embracing all the challenges and working hard to make the world a better place. I live and breathe that each day."

CHAPTER 8

FROM OPENNESS TO RADICAL TRANSPARENCY TO UNPRECEDENTED LEVELS OF ACCESSIBILITY

It is a sad fact that most systems are closed. Perhaps parts of a system operate as open, but this is often on a very limited scale. This is true for political, corporate, and public leadership alike.

Our systems are largely closed as a defense mechanism against those who believe differently from us about things like policies, culture, or language. Over time, if we play defense long enough, we put that defense into policy and embed it within our culture.

Many organizational cultures have evolved around power dynamics, which also reinforce a closed system. When this happens, not knowing an answer becomes an opportunity to be outdone.

In the new language of leadership we are building here, when there are winners and losers (think competence), there will almost never be learners. We strive for open but live for closed. This is the single greatest obstacle of being on a path of continuous improvement in all that we do, whether personally or professionally. Why is it so easy to create and maintain a closed system and so very difficult to create and maintain an open system?

Perhaps it is best to start with why you, as an individual, are likely a closed system.

We all have a reactive orientation to the current reality we face. It is a default human setting—and it is easy to understand from a physical perspective. When we start to feel cold, we find many strategies to warm up (eating a hot cup of soup, putting on a sweater, sitting by the fire, turning up the thermostat). This is true for many of the systems of the body, including the mind. The reactive orientation often manifests covertly in our assumptions and thinking models. When we see something, learn something, or are challenged by something, we react from our current state.

For most of us, this reaction is present in just a few archetypes: defense, acceptance, or inquiry.

We have already discussed the move from closed and knowing into open and learning within this new leadership language. This movement is largely focused on self. When we are closed and knowing and a challenge arises, we have a choice to defend our thinking (to be judgmental), simply accept new thinking, or be curious and inquisitive (to seek understanding). The movement within the self towards open and learning is a movement toward self-inquiry. This chapter takes the idea of inquiry to the next level beyond self and into our teams, organizations, and communities.

The Open, Learning Self

Self-inquiry leads to a better sense of self and position. We must be grounded and thoughtful about our assumptions to have a firm base from which to form our opinions. This collective inquiry is a step towards understanding others by focusing on those around us in any size group of more than one. It is imperative that the self is open and learning for collective inquiry to have any hope of success.

If an individual moves into collective inquiry thinking and they have the answer or know best, the experience is no longer inquiry but more like interrogation. If self is open, collective inquiry allows for us to focus on other and ask, "What is it this person believes to be true and what are the guiding questions?" There should be a back-and-forth of sharing assumptions and beliefs, devoid of judgement. This is easy with friends and those who believe as we do. Being open and learning, or accepting of new ideas, is a relatively easy concept to grasp.

When a friend suggests something, we are prone to dialogue and discussion to find resolution. As Peter M. Senge writes in *The Fifth Discipline: The Art and Practice of the Learning Organization*, "A learning team masters movement back and forth between dialogue and discussion. The ground rules are different. The goals are different. Failing to distinguish them, teams usually have neither dialogue nor productive discussions" (Ch. 12). Senge specifically differentiates between dialogue as seeking to understand and discussion as seeking to persuade. (I have greatly over-generalized what he writes, and I encourage you to check it out to understand his thinking more deeply.)

Let us examine a hypothetical situation with a well-intentioned but not fully open manager who has read the leadership language handbook and has a deeper understanding. Eager to try this new language of leadership, they find themselves on Monday morning with a new sales recruit as part of an onboarding session. Let's drop in on part of the conversation.

Manager: *Welcome! I am glad to have you on board and look forward to spending the next few minutes with you.*

Recruit: *I'm excited to be a part of the team. I've had some sales success in the past and look forward to applying it here.*

Manager: *Excellent, I'm glad to hear that. We are an open*

and learning culture around here, so I have no doubt you will love it.

Recruit: *That sounds great, I cannot say I have always worked in an open and learning culture, so I am eager to learn more.*

Manager: *I've been in this company for 20 years and have risen through the ranks. If there is one thing we can always count on, it's change! To that end, I have dealt with just about every major sales crisis you can imagine, so please don't hesitate to stop in anytime you have questions. After all, we are a learning culture!*

But are we? Read that last paragraph again and ask yourself two important questions. First, did the manager say they are a learning culture? Yes. Did the manager communicate to the recruit that they are a learning culture? Decidedly no. The manager communicated that they had answers. They communicated expertise. They communicated competence. They communicated closed and knowing. Imagine that the final paragraph were to read differently.

Manager: *I have been in this company for 20 years and have risen through the ranks. If there is one thing we can always count on, it's change! To that end, I have identified a growth opportunity for our culture and for me professionally, and that is discovering new techniques for utilizing our current customer base to gather references. I'm curious what has worked for you in the past, and what have you always wanted to try?*

Did the manager tell the recruit they are a learning culture? Not exactly, and not overtly. Did the manager communicate they are open and learning? Absolutely. Note, that manager shared suffering (compassion). By leading with vulnerability, the manager created a safe space for the new recruit to live in a world of vulnerability.

Think of the number of new employees your organization onboards every year. Regardless of your industry, I can assure you most organizations say they are open and learning but communicate closed and knowing. This may seem trivial—but think of the lost opportunities, from a warehouse floor where a new employee spots a previously unknown danger to a new teacher who has not yet mastered the craft to a new manager who is unsteady in their position. Over and over again, we reinforce a covert culture of closed and knowing, simply by the language of competence we chose to use.

Let us turn our attention to one-on-one conversations with those who think differently to make this more real. Think of a difficult conversation with someone around religion, politics, sex, or money as an example—someone whose strongly held beliefs challenge your own.

If conversations with that individual have been hard in the past, this new approach may seem nearly impossible at first. The idea of being open and learning is largely a foreign concept to these conversations. If we are being honest with ourselves, we recognize that we move into a defensive position with the idea ... and ultimately, with the person. We may feel a defensive position is a required state to defend our beliefs and assumptions.

A good first step is to go on offense. This does not mean offense in the form of attacking their position but rather playing offense with the idea. This takes the form of "what if" and "I wonder" questions. Asking something like, "I wonder what parts of this idea relate to my way of understanding the world?" is an example of offense. Playing offense with ideas allows us to play offense more easily with the person we are speaking with. "Help me understand" is a sentence designed for collective inquiry. Using this example, an expert leader can not just engage in self-inquiry, but lead others to do the same. There are myriad ways to do this, of course. When it fails, it is usually because the leader is not guiding others through self-inquiry but is simply challenging beliefs.

To understand better, think of basketball practice. To improve, we must practice skills like dribbling and shooting and passing individually. The previous chapters of this book have shown you language you can use to improve your skills. These are a series of skills that can eventually be strung together in a conversation, just like ball handling skills in a basketball game.

Very soon, it becomes imperative to string these skills together by practicing with one another. Think of a game of one-on-one. Ideally, the other person has also practiced these skills, and when they are on offense, you are on defense. When you are on offense, they are on defense. It is oppositional by nature.

Learning to play as a team matches our skills and commonalities towards a greater purpose. This is also the secret to collective inquiry. The greater purpose is not to win but to understand.

We introduced the concept of purposeful "strange making" earlier in the book, and this skill becomes very helpful at this turn. Making an entire situation strange requires the ability to stand above the play of action and see where our efforts are aligned and where they may be misaligned. Making strange requires a suspension of our beliefs. When you deeply understand another, you can easily accept the reality of their beliefs. Accepting does not mean agreeing, it simply means accepting. By accepting an idea as true, we are more easily able to play with that idea. We can inquire and deliberate. We can also find commonalities in our play.

There is always an opportunity to find something in the argument you can agree with, a common denominator. It may be a phrase like this: "I can see you are very passionate about this, and I appreciate that. I have also noticed that we both believe something must be done about …." This is the turn.

Appreciation Turns into Affiliation

A movement from self-inquiry to collective inquiry is a good first step, but it is just the first part of our turn. The second part is to move from collective inquiry to reflective inquiry. This is how we transform appreciation into affiliation and affiliation into action.

This transformation can only happen after we have achieved collective inquiry, which comes in the form of turning our attention back on ourselves. Once you deeply understand the other person's views and beliefs, you must challenge your own. You must wonder why you believe what you do and whether your beliefs are misguided.

Using the example of the basketball team, reflective inquiry can come after a play or at the final buzzer of the game. "I wonder if my efforts supported the team when ..." is an example. "What deficits did I see within myself?" is another. Those versed in grassroots politics will recognize the formula of "my story, your story, our story." Self-to-collective-to-reflective is telling our story, hearing another's story, and forging a synthesis of both.

To this point, we have focused on individuals and small teams. This work is difficult—and, by its very definition, learning a new language requires the deliberate practice of conversing with someone else in the language. This is where a good leadership coach can be invaluable.

I have always believed the essence of good coaching is a process. This is true for athletic coaching, skill coaching, leadership coaching, and organizational coaching. The level of specificity in your gap analysis plan will determine both the focus and quality of your practice, and it is the best predictor of future performance.

Most of us, when practicing collective inquiry, have a massive gap between where we want to be and where we start. We need a coach to help us define, in granular detail, the difference between what we do currently and what we want to do. We must master this leadership language on the individual scale in order to have any hope of success on the organizational level. Further, a coach gives you a practice field. Would a musician ever step on stage without practicing? Of course not. Neither would an athlete. Neither should a leader. We need to find practice courts and a practice squad for our leadership if we are going to have any real chance of finding success.

Organizational Proprioception

Organizational leadership has changed since the industrial revolution. Most organizations, as a functional aspect of their business, have largely moved away from categorization and into integration as a framework. This move is starting to bear fruit in terms of how we think about our human resource function as well. This concept is how we scale self-inquiry, collective inquiry, and reflective inquiry within—and outside of—our organizations.

To master the new language of leadership, we must pivot our thinking from focusing on individuals to focusing on interactions between individuals. This is an opportunity to connect what we've covered in previous chapters:

- Mastering the new language of leadership means you inherently see hierarchies as an establishment of power dynamics.
- Power dynamics are a defense strategy that brings our focus to individuals rather than interactions.
- The evolved leader recognizes we move from hierarchies into networks.
- Networks focus on interactions first.
- Networks build collective and reflective inquiry.
- Networks are non-fragile, whereas hierarchies are very fragile.

Let us also quickly connect excuse and explain. As you will recall, excuse is competency-based, fragile, and focused on self. Explanation is focused on others. It is inquiry based, and non-fragile.

Your ability to be antifragile as a leader and to build a non-fragile organization requires vulnerability at the highest levels. This vulnerability comes not just from you, the leader, but from the organization itself, because if you are deeply connected to what is deep inside you, it provides a confidence bordering on fearlessness toward being vulnerable.

You could build mountains from the books written on finding self-purpose or discovering your personal why. You could build even bigger mountains from books that offer the same for organizations. These books are a critical resource for you in understanding the context of being truly vulnerable.

Radical Transparency

Radical transparency requires openness not just with parts of your system but at its core. A good working definition is simply unprecedented levels of accessibility to both people and information.

Let's use a mental image of how a leader develops and lives this concept.

Imagine an individual who is moving from one aspect of a company to another or to an entirely new organization. Perhaps they are moving up in their career. Either way, there is movement towards something new and unknown. There will be new teams, new projects, new bosses, new goals, new ways of getting work done, new policies, new expectations, and on and on. It is all new and it is all overwhelming.

It can feel tremendously disorienting, like being caught in a hurricane.

Successful leaders often struggle through these types of transitions. In order to understand why this happens, let's turn to a different mental model. Proprioception is the internal knowledge of where your body is in space. If I ask you to close your eyes and take your index finger and touch it to your nose, nearly all of you would be able to do it. This is proprioception. The better your accuracy, the better your proprioception. This is why people get seasick. They feel their body move through space but have a fundamental understanding they are not moving their body. The brain interprets this to mean you have ingested a poison, and you feel nauseous in order to remove the poison from your body.

Now imagine not having any idea where your feet or hands are. Over time, leaders develop an organizational proprioception, whether they're on small teams or within large organizations. They know how to access certain elements or where other people are working almost intuitively. They are able to see around corners and predict behavior. All of this is simply organizational proprioception.

When leaders enter a new position or organization, they lose proprioception. The natural reaction to this disorientation is to do what we have always done to stabilize our bodies in order to stop the feeling or, perhaps unconsciously, to fight to get rid of the poison. Does that transition feel closed or open?

This is obviously a closed response. In our experience, 99 out of 100 leaders will lose organizational proprioception and become closed and knowing. This limits their learning and effectiveness and, worse, it self-reinforces the system itself to remain closed.

If we truly want open systems, it starts with leadership. You must be wondering how a leader can move from one organization to another without losing orientation ... and the answer is purpose, self-realization, and radical transparency. Radical transparency finds the leader sharing their vulnerability on the very first day in the very first meeting. A leader who has undergone self-inquiry will already be aware that they are disoriented and will be more receptive to collaborative inquiry, asking themselves how this new way of thinking accords with their previous way of thinking.

The leader also takes this opportunity to engage the new team in questioning why they do what they do and asking for their help in understanding. Finally, the master leader of this new language is able to take the entire team into reflective inquiry. *I wonder if we can ....*

But far too often, this never happens. The newly appointed leader is closed—and that is where the story ends. We read about vulnerability, and it seems so simple. In truth, real vulnerability is a superpower.

Will you be a master of this language the first time you try? Of course not. You will make mistakes. You will suffer. You will share your suffering with others, and they will help you. This is how we develop mastery. If you really want a deep understanding of mastery, you must recognize the true master has failed more times than the novice has even tried.

TRANSFORMATIONAL LEADERSHIP IN PRACTICE

BILL McCULLOUGH

VP Sales, Education Technology

Growing up, Bill McCullough traveled with his family to Indiana each summer for an annual family reunion. He particularly loved spending time with his older cousins, whom he looked up to and really admired. But one summer, when Bill was just 14, he got a call from his older cousin, Joey, who told him he wasn't going to come to the family reunion that year.

"I remember talking to him for about an hour that day, and I said, 'Oh, come on, you're only an hour away, just come!'" Bill said. "But that was the last time I spoke to Joey. He killed himself later that night."

Bill has never forgotten that conversation. He doesn't recall any signs that he should have caught—and at just 14, he had no idea what to be listening for that day. "That has weighed heavily on me. At Joey's funeral, they asked the eldest of each of the six family's children to be pallbearers, and I refused to do it because I was so upset. I always felt guilty about not being able to save him."

When Bill had an opportunity to spend his career saving kids' lives, he jumped at the chance. He was so committed to his role that he considered it his life's mission. "I told them I didn't even care what they paid me. I accepted the role before even knowing the salary because I felt compelled to save the future Joey's of the world."

Finding Strength Through Vulnerability

But Bill didn't offer his "why" to his new employer. "I didn't even tell that story to my wife until a few years after I was in my role," he admitted.

When Bill finally let his boss know about Joey, he encouraged Bill to share the story with his team to build trust and reciprocity. When he finally did, "there wasn't a dry eye in the room," Bill recalled. "But this didn't come without my questioning whether I was ready to be that vulnerable in front of my team."

In the end, he felt compelled to talk about his dedication to the opportunity to save children's lives every single day. He believes this transformed his role as a leader as well as his relationship with his team. He realizes now that "if you can be vulnerable and share some of the burdens you're carrying and your personal reason for why you are doing what you do, it can be incredibly powerful. I have never felt so close to my team. They all thanked me so much for sharing this.

"There's a lot of talk about starting with why," Bill said, "but it really was the 'why' for me that made it so I could not do anything else but go out there and save as many kids as humanly possible."

Start with the 'Why' and the Results Will Follow

It may seem like a "soft" approach to lead with compassion and vulnerability, but Bill found this has actually contributed to his company's success. Achieving annual records seven years in a row is, Bill believes, a direct result of his staying mission oriented. Instead of congratulating a colleague on a $100,000 deal, his coworkers congratulate them on protecting 20,000 children from harm.

They talk about everything they do (even on the sales teams) in terms of the lives of children. "We found that if you keep pushing the why, rather than the money and the quotas, you get a much better response out of your people. I've led many, many teams in the last 30 years, and I've never been so mission focused. It's been incredibly powerful," Bill said.

"This mission led me to change things from numbers to stuff that matters. I don't care whether you sell cars or pencils, if you can get it down to why it matters and focus your team's attention fully on that, you're going to get more out of them," he said. "I encourage leaders who may not have a mission as profound as protecting children to consider why you do what you do? Spend less time in reports and more time with people. Why do your people do what they do? Focus on that. Don't focus on the numbers; the numbers will come."

Asking for Help Is a Sign of Strength

Bill believes that asking for help is a sign of strength, not a sign of weakness, and that mental health is important. "I have seen a therapist, and I'm not embarrassed to say that. I'm proud to say it," he said. "It helps keep me motivated and grounded. Seeking someone in your life that can help keep you stay grounded is very, very important.

"There are days where this job is horrible," he continued. "Anytime you're a leader in sales, you're going to have bad days and good days. If you're not taking care of yourself, it's going to be more difficult to love and celebrate the successes and failures with your team."

He reinforces this by meeting with an executive coach every other week. "I've been in sales for 30 years, so when I tell some people I have a coach, they're like, 'What possibly can you learn from your coach after all of these years?' Well, Tiger Woods has a coach. Any performer, they have a coach. So who am I not to have a coach?'" He says his coach helps him continue to stay grounded, focus on the things that he may have missed, and improve as a leader.

Deflect Praise and Absorb Criticism

Bill has always had two simple rules when he leads. The first rule is to love your people, and the second is to deflect praise and absorb criticism. He maintains that "if something great happens, it's because of the team's effort," not because of his leadership. "If something goes wrong, it's because I didn't communicate clearly. Or maybe I did not make sure that they understood what I was talking about," he said.

"I never use the words 'my team'—it's our team—and I also never use the word 'manager.' I hate that word. People hate being managed, but they like being led. I believe in being a leader and not a manager," he said. "I think if you do those things, people will realize, 'Wow, he is in the boat with me, and I'm in the boat, too, and I'm rowing as furiously as I can to help us get to that destination.' I'm not just yelling, 'Stroke! And you guys go and do it.'"

Ask More Questions (and Listen to the Answers!)

Bill believes that learning about workers as individuals should start very early in the interview process. "You should be figuring out what lights a fire under this person. What do they get excited about?" he advised. "That's part of learning about them as a human being. This means asking good questions, like where do they want to be and what inspires them to do what they do every day?"

"I want to work with our team to solve problems, and the first way to do that, is to start asking questions, not making demands. I ask them, 'If you were running the show, what would you do? If you were going to invent the next version of the sales team, what would you do differently?'" He continued, "Don't ask questions that put people on the spot, but encourage them to think creatively. 'If you were going to design the next version of whatever product you might have, what would you design?' Once you start asking these questions, you will see them start to think more creatively."

At Education Technology, collective thinking is a key component to teams' success, and Bill encourages other leaders to consider adopting that approach as well, because when people feel like they are contributing to the solution, there's no need to try to get buy-in. They are owners in the solution. "Whenever we have a difficult problem, rather than sit in my ivory tower and try to figure it out, the first thing I do is call people and share that this problem has been presented to us and ask them what we should do about it," he said. "Then I shut up and listen."

Applying Radical Transparency to Increase Engagement

Bill believes in being transparent—not just about clients and the challenges they are dealing with to support students, but also from a leadership perspective. "If you are having meetings, you need to be radically transparent in those meetings about what you're struggling with—and, from a corporate perspective, what we're struggling with," he advised.

"One of the things that we do in our executive meetings is end every meeting with takeaways on what we are going to bring back to our teams and tell them that we've accomplished in this meeting or what we're struggling with in this meeting. That means that every time executives meet, other people in the company understand exactly what we're struggling with at the top."

One recent example was the challenge of infusing company culture into a remote environment. "We let them know that as leaders, we're struggling with this," Bill said. "We posed the question to our teams: 'What do you suggest?' That's being radically transparent because you're being vulnerable and admitting you don't have all the answers and you're asking for help.

"If you can do that, you will be amazed at how your people will connect with you. I always say, individually, we don't have all the answers—but collectively, we do. The problem as leaders is we feel that because we're being paid the most, we need to solve the problem," he said. "If you can get the collective engaged, chances are you're going to solve it correctly the first time. Being transparent is a huge part of that."

Don't Be Afraid to Get Crazy

Bill believes in trying completely odd (even crazy) things to see if they just might work to solve a problem. In a previous role, Bill was asked to lead an inbound sales team that sold five different products. They had individuals specialized in each one of the five disciplines. But he started noticing that during certain periods of the day, people were on hold way too long, so he invited the entire team to train on all of the five disciplines.

"Now, this was a lot of work, but it provided variety for their job, and the team liked it," he said. "They found that if one of the products was slow, they could work on one of the others, and it enabled us to get to our customers more efficiently. They went from a call abandonment rate of 20% to an abandonment rate of a fraction of 1%, and 99.9% of calls were answered in 20 seconds instead of just 50%. This all worked without increasing headcount."

Bill also had a similar experience in his current role where the company was losing funding for one of their products within the first six months of his arrival on the job. "I had to strip down the entire sales force and start over. Yes, that did provide a little angst for a short amount of time until we got through it. But once we did, it set off seven years in a row of record numbers. Do not be afraid to tear everything down and try something new."

One final piece of Bill's advice is a common mistake he sees with new leaders. "Don't try to create another Bill McCullough. Most leaders are put in a position of leadership because they've done their job very, very well, and so they think, if I could just create more of me, then we would get the job done. Try to help them to be the best Katie, the best Sarah, and the best Tommy they can be. Don't try to recreate yourself, and once again, that requires really taking the time to get to know your team as individuals, their strengths, and weaknesses, to help them achieve their full potential."

CHAPTER 9

FROM ENGAGEMENT TO OWNERSHIP COMMITMENT TO DISCIPLINE

We have arrived at the place where we bring everything together. If you approach your leadership work as complicated/competent, you will plan, you will direct, you will tell people what you want from them, you will get excuses, and you will work hard for engagement or buy-in. It's not a matter of if you will find yourself in hot water, it is a matter of when. Buy-in and engagement need to be buried and never resurrected.

If, on the other hand, you approach leadership within the framework of complex/compassionate, you will find nuance, you will seek out, you will tell people what you want for them, you will get explanations, and people will give you ownership. They will own these problems with you. Ownership around the complex is antifragile. Out of chaos, we do not get disorder and confusion. Out of chaos, we gain order. We become indestructible.

The mental pivot requires a shift in focus for the leader from finding the right solution towards asking the right question.

Picture something you own (a house, a car, etc.). As an owner, you might or might not take care of this item, but are you frequently judging your competence? Generally, the answer is no. The same is true for ideas. If you don't believe me, talk to anyone who has created a weight management plan that has worked for several years, and you will realize they own the mindset. They didn't buy in or engage. If they did, the program would have failed. People who own their personal finances rarely, if ever, have a problem. Employees who own the business have a completely different orientation to their work.

The truth is, this whole book has been about change management. This can be personal, professional, or organizational.

What is the biggest resistance to change? Most often, it is the system itself. Systems are designed to get the outcomes they are designed to get. They are self-reinforcing. Change management is the recognition that a leader must be a systems architect.

We design systems around a collective vision through relationships.

Equally important to change management is the

differentiation between technical solutions and adaptive solutions (based on the work of Ron Heifitz and Marty Linskey). Much of what is presented to leadership is presented as technical, when in fact, it might be adaptive. Technical problems have technical solutions.

As you connect what you've learned in this book, you should already be thinking, "Technical problems are complicated!" Adaptive problems, however, are like the carnival game Whack-a-Mole. You solve one problem, and it re-presents similarly somewhere else. All these secondary problems lead to a larger, culturally adaptive problem: resistance to change.

And now you're thinking, "Adaptive problems are complex!" You've got it. Should we use the same language and framework to solve technical and adaptive problems? Absolutely not. But many do just that.

This means we must talk about our problems very publicly and excitedly. As we've discovered, most organizational cultures are set up to resist any kind of real change because people are afraid of blame. Leaders in virtually every corporate or public culture say they want to innovate, but they often live in a culture of judgement and blame. The outcome, people, and leaders themselves are up for judgement, and judgment is ALL about competence.

Competence leadership kills innovation culture, and change dies with it. Competence leadership gets excuses over explanations. Competence is all about the leader telling everyone what they want from them. Competence is what makes our organizations fragile.

Throughout this book, we have referenced Nassim Nicholas Taleb's *Antifragile: Things That Gain from Disorder*. His work has nothing to do with change management, but it is critical for understanding how to manage change. To become antifragile, we must move away from competence-based leadership and into compassionate leadership—which, as you'll recall from the opening chapter, means "to suffer with."

To recap: We build culture around collective suffering. We do not judge when leading a compassionate organization. We don't get excuses, but we get a lot of explanations. This helps us move away from telling people what we want from them and allows us to talk freely about what we want for them. This is the bedrock for change and innovation.

You are no doubt wondering if this actually works. It does. The biggest positive from our work is the conceptual shift in leadership that we have described and are starting to see throughout the country. Once the new language of leadership has become part of the culture and architecture of the organization, change is more readily accepted, and we have a shared future.

Commitment to Discipline

Finally, you might be saying, "I am ready to commit to this new language of leadership." Please do not. In fact, we encourage you to consider suspending your use of the term "commitment." A commitment is something you do without giving a lot of thought to it. Since we have used exercise and nutrition throughout this book to make concepts more easily understood, let's do it one final time.

If you commit to an exercise regimen, you will follow it every day without deviation. Right up until you don't. Commitment is irrevocable. When we break a commitment, we invite self-critical judgement. If your commitment is to run ten miles per day, six days per week, that is what you do. And then when you don't, you have broken this commitment to yourself. Judgement ensues, along with excuses, self-pity, and sometimes failure.

Fragility is inherent in the word commitment in part because of what it conjures up in our minds. We all know couples who have divorced. We may have had friendships dissolve. Commitment might work, but it also might fail.

So please do not commit to this new language of leadership. Instead, let's talk about discipline. The Latin origin of discipline is "instruction" or "knowledge." It's about teaching and learning. For example, it takes discipline to learn how to play an instrument or to learn a new language. A disciplined runner might say, "I ran ten miles six days per week in my thirties, but my body has changed and now I run eight miles three times per week." Being disciplined is knowing things change over time—and so should your practice.

A disciplined spouse is in a constant state of non-critical analysis of the relationship and the self. What has changed? What has stayed the same? What can be improved? These allow for explanations over excuses. Being disciplined in our friendships means the same thing. Relationships based on discipline become much deeper and much more fulfilling.

An organization might be committed to mentoring but strive to be disciplined about sponsoring. Or it might be committed to its hierarchy but have a long way to grow in order to be disciplined about its networks. Perhaps its leaders are committed to what they want from people but could be disciplined about what they want for people. Nearly every company is committed to feedback, and a growing number are disciplined about feed-forward.

Imagine a workplace that moves from being committed about fitting in to being disciplined about belonging. Or moves from committed to openness to disciplined about radical transparency. Or moves from committed to management to disciplined about leadership.

Have we just described the ideal work environment? If so, what's stopping you?

In a nutshell:

- You were trained and schooled for a world that is quickly disappearing.
- What got you here won't get you there.

- The old paradigm was built around speaking as leading.
- The new paradigm recognizes leadership as multidimensional and requires different skill sets and language for each dimension.
- If unconditional faith is lost, your journey is over.
- Replacing the old paradigms with new ones is deeply painful—and absolutely critical.
- The old paradigm meant leadership came up with solutions.
- The new paradigm means leadership is learning how to ask new questions in new ways.
- Exploring this new leadership forces us to see the familiar through a new frame and demands that we become the best version of ourselves in the process.
- The new leadership is dependent on the leader's ongoing exploration, learning, and development.

TRANSFORMATIONAL LEADERSHIP IN PRACTICE

DAVE MacLEOD

Co-Founder and CEO, ThoughtExchange

Dave MacLeod did not set out to be a technologist. As the son of two special education school teachers, he became immersed in the world of community development from a young age.

"I was a person who went to all sorts of universities and took all sorts of classes and got exactly zero degrees," he said. "Many of my school counselors would say, 'You know that philosophy and astronomy and political science and magazine art don't add up to a degree?' Instead, I was fascinated by community development and how decisions could be affected by facilitating a group of people and community members."

In particular, Dave was interested in decision-making that positively affected outcomes—and how community funding was involved. He began to question how that was achievable and the generative way of understanding what a community wants rather than relying on companies and individuals to come up with ideas and then "sell their people on it."

"I started to do more and more large face-to-face events and gatherings of ten, fifty, or two hundred people, and along the way I learned a lot about bias—particularly the bias a consultant can bring into a group setting. If you're the person gathering people's thoughts, interpreting what others are saying, and identifying the themes, you hold a lot of power in determining the outcomes of those meetings," he said.

So Dave began to hone strategies to eliminate some of this bias. He came across a game called "35." The idea was simple: To learn what a group values, ask an open-ended question and give each player a recipe card or sticky note to write down their answers without signing their name. Next, shuffle the cards and distribute them around the room via players exchanging cards with one another until they are told to stop. Then each person looks at their card and rates the idea on a scale of seven. The shuffling and rating happened five times. At the end of the game, the facilitator collects the cards and counts backwards from thirty-five to find the highest-rated cards, forming the discussion agenda based on these items.

This transparent process reveals what matters to the group without allowing any participants to disproportionately affect the event by hijacking the agenda or overbearing the conversation. Everyone feels included in the process and deems it to be fair.

Dave found that people loved this approach and the outcomes. But ultimately, he began to realize that one of the biggest determiners of those outcomes was who was in the room.

"It turns out that most of community development is marketing—and the outcomes were only as good as how many people we could actually get to come and participate," he explained. "I found that we would run all these well-meaning events, and we would say that we were going to gather the community, but who would show up? We would get 15 people who were all predominantly white and who all had some sort of privilege that allowed them to be able to come and attend a big group gathering."

Among their commonalities: They were not working or had a flexible work schedule. They had decided this was a priority. They enjoyed large gatherings. They felt it was safe for them to attend. "That's a small percentage of the population," Dave pointed out.

"Yet these individuals were the ones deciding on the future of whatever it was that would impact everyone."

A friend of Dave's named Lee White was intrigued by his approach to community development and collecting feedback with recipe cards. Lee said it reminded him of what his friend, Jim Firstbrook, was building. At the time, Jim was a product manager for a large printing pre-press called CREO.

"Jim was a physicist and an engineer," Dave recalled, "and Lee told me he was creating intelligence software. I was like, 'What the hell is that?' I was definitely not interested in software, and Jim thought I was this flaky guy running around doing community development with sticky notes and flip cards, so he was not interested in me. However, through the perseverance of our friend Lee, we ended up meeting, and I had a chance to see the very first demo of what was ThoughtStream at the time.

"I immediately recognized this would solve the biggest problem in community development: Who's in the room? I realized that technology could actually play a major role in how we scale and have conversations in business or in communities. It's a big idea to take this face-to-face modality and digitize it. That was a big concept for me, and from there we created ThoughtExchange."

Operationalizing Empathy and Compassion

As a company, ThoughtExchange has been exploring possible ways to operationalize the programmatic side of empathy and compassion for more than a decade. "What I mean by operationalizing this process is thinking about what your actual business practice is to ensure that you're reaching out and learning from people about the decisions that affect them," Dave explained. "How would you not only articulate that as a value, but then demonstrate the practice that you undertake in order to actually do it? When you look at your day-to-day operations, what are those moments that you are meaningfully and intentionally listening to people, understanding their perspectives, and bringing that in to be able to drive your business forward? And how do you communicate that back out to your teams?"

Dave gave the following example of how ThoughtExchange might talk internally about compassion. 'We have a fully compassionate organization because here's all the evidence and here's the business process that we have to actually operationalize it.' I realize that sounds like a pretty dry way to think about compassion, but actually creating an operationalized structure around empathy and compassion has been a priority for us," he said. "Listening is the only way to actually achieve it, versus just talking about it as a priority and not understanding how to actually do it."

When ThoughtExchange invites the perspective of the whole company, its leaders know they're getting the perspectives of 100 percent of its workforce. "This means that when a quarter closes, we want to understand the successes and actions everyone feels we need to take—and then we determine how we respond to that information," Dave said. "We bring it into our corporate decision-making."

As Humans, By Our Very Nature, We Are Vulnerable

The ThoughtExchange senior leadership team connects regularly with a third-party moderator to discuss how they are doing professionally, how they're doing personally, and how they show up as full 360-degree humans who encourage radical transparency in how they lead and support their teams.

"As an example," Dave said, "I'm really proud of our group for taking on gender bias and gathering 30 senior managers to spend a half day talking about shared experience as it relates to gender bias in the workplace and what needs to be done to overcome it. It's a pretty vulnerable topic. It's messy, and it's not easy to go through. It would be easier to just say, 'We're working on it' but not actually do anything about it."

To clarify, Dave does not believe vulnerability is a thing you do. Rather, he believes it's an acceptance of the reality of yourself. "People talk about vulnerability as a practice. I'm going to be vulnerable. No, you're going to have to accept your vulnerability; you are vulnerable already. Humans are vulnerable. It's a matter of how we choose to deal with our vulnerability that has the biggest implication on our leadership."

He doesn't equate vulnerability with having had difficult experiences in the past. "If you get beaten up by a thing that happened to you, there was a consequence, and you need to deal with that. You can show up in deep empathy. You can cry, express it through communication, and share emotions and true connection. Or you can avoid a conversation, shut down, and maybe even end up in harmful behaviors such as excessive alcohol consumption. But even that consequence might cause you to tap a behavior shift," he said.

"I think we get to choose how we express our vulnerability, and people need to talk about healthy expressions of vulnerability versus less healthy expressions of vulnerability—but you don't get to choose to be vulnerable."

Using the Complex and the Complicated to Inform Decisions

Through the millions of people participating in decision analysis of learning, Dave has discovered that when it comes to decision-making and gathering input, there are actually two ways to involve people in the complex and in the complicated. "If you are looking for a big-picture perspective from every single person within an organization—and one of our clients has just over 679,000 employees—there is actually a question you can ask everyone: "What are some perspectives that you believe are really important for us to consider as we're making decisions?"

This question works for several reasons, Dave explained. "Even if someone just started yesterday, they have a perspective on why they joined the organization and what they believe to be important. That is a question that you can scale and ask any organization in the world."

However, there is a key caveat to this approach. Despite the value of collective feedback, Dave does not believe these questions should be used to democratize decision-making. "Part of complex decision-making is gathering perspectives to understand them to better inform decisions. It's not about saying, 'Let's vote on everything because then we're going to make the best decisions,'" he said.

He also has a deep appreciation for experts, "those who are immersed in the complicated, to get their recommendations for actions that can be taken," Dave said. "Tapping into these experts can be incredibly beneficial. For example, in an organization where you have teachers, you have experts on students, you have parents who are experts on kids, and there are kids who are experts on their own education. How do you reach out to those people to ask them questions about the complicated to understand exactly what they need based on their lived experience? You can actually go to people in the complicated and ask them for tactical solutions, respecting their authority as the professionals, to help solve the problem and inform decision-making."

He continued, "One of our prouder moments at ThoughtExchange was a notable study we conducted where we compared direct student feedback to some of the best-practice research coming out of the world's leading universities. We went directly to tenth-grade students and asked them what would make their education more valuable and relevant. They shared that they would like to see facilitated learning, technology as an enabler of education (but not a replacement), and adaptive learning technologies available so that they can move quickly through content they already know and spend more time on what they still need to master."

Remarkably, these students identified research coming out of the universities as best practice recommendations. "I don't want to take away from the years of research that was conducted to amass the studies released by these universities about what students need," Dave cautioned, "but it's incredibly powerful to be able to just go ask a thousand students, and in minutes, they'll tell you what they need and want. And their feedback maps almost perfectly to those studies because students are the experts on themselves. They're in the complicated—and if you ask them a question, they actually do know the answer, and will tell you what they need. We just need to ask."

The Transformation Starts with Discomfort

Dave knows that most people don't seek out input from their organization to disrupt their thinking. Typically, he believes, it's more likely that leaders are looking to affirm their biases and reinforce the decisions they are already planning to make. It can be challenging when that doesn't happen.

"When you get your bias affirmed through collective feedback, and the outcome is exactly what you anticipated, it's like you're playing Candy Crush or scrolling Instagram," he said. "It gives you that dopamine hit: 'See, I was right.'

"The flip side is when your bias is challenged. Studies have suggested you can, in fact, experience sensations of discomfort in your brain, as well as the desire to fight, flight, or flee, which is deeply ingrained in the human experience.

"Therefore," he continued, "there's an opportunity to feel the triggered moment and say, 'Oh, I have some learning to do, and this pain is teaching me something that I don't understand.' When leaders enter that moment of feeling oddly defensive, if they can recognize that it's a fight, flight, or flee mechanism that is being triggered, because their bias is being challenged, they have an opportunity to take a moment to allow the cycle to complete to see the full transformation."

However, Dave added on a cautionary note, "When you think you know better than the collective input of your team or your organization, and you interrupt the cycle halfway, you are in dangerous territory. Believe me, there are many leaders who do things like quote Steve Jobs and Henry Ford and suggest that if Henry Ford would have listened to his customers, he would have just made a better horse.

"I think if Henry Ford had a way to actually tap into the collective and understand that they wanted to accelerate, he probably would have skipped right to the electric car," Dave said. "If they figured out what humans really wanted, we wouldn't have built everything up with carbon, so I refute this idea that listening to your customers would have just created endless horses."

"As humans," Dave reflected, "we often let the pain of getting our bias challenged dictate our behavior for months, weeks, years, or sometimes to death, unfortunately. If we're able to take a moment and digest the feedback, however long it takes to accelerate our competency on that issue, there is an opportunity to create true transformation."

Putting This into Action with Ownership and Accountability

ThoughtExchange has created a unique, real-time, bias-free business process to make sure they are tapping into their collective to regularly enlist feedback. Even more importantly, though, they now have a process for taking this feedback and putting it into action, essentially holding themselves accountable for responding to what their team wants and needs.

"We recently collected insights from our organization about things we can do to improve," Dave said. "One of the comments that was shared is, 'You have to stop asking this question until you're willing to actually take action based on our feedback.'"

The leaders replied with alacrity. "We were able to respond with the action steps we took following the last time we did this, in addition to a few more updates that were not even on the list. It was a very thorough, well thought out, accountable action list. People just hadn't followed on to that next step, so when we communicated that we were indeed holding ourselves accountable, it was a powerful moment," Dave said.

"We're now just starting to get good at not only asking the right questions, but also taking action to address the collective feedback," he continued. "This means considering how we can take meaningful action that's really going to solve the problem as well as how we are communicating that back in a way that it can operationalize the programmatic side. If this is done well, people will start to see that this organization believes in its people so much that it has actually created a framework of success based on the input of their individuals. We will fail at this goal proudly for the next 10 years, I'm sure, because it's so hard when the bar is set this high—but that high bar is where we want to be."

WHAT'S NEXT?

Are you ready to put your learning into practice? If you're anything like us, this book has inspired you to take the next step of your journey toward becoming a more compassionate leader. You realize that leadership is changing, and you are ready to learn the framework for mapping out how, why, and what this looks like in practice.

In our course "Transformational Leadership in Practice," you will hear from leaders who are applying this framework within their own organizations and how it has transformed their teams for their better.

At the end of the course, you will have an opportunity to pursue a compassionate leadership certification and to join a community of peers who are all in the pursuit of their own language of leadership that celebrates and empowers those around them.

Join us! **http://transformationalleadershipsecret.com**

NOTES

Chapter 1

"Leadership." (n.d.). In *Meriam-Webster's online dictionary*. Retrieved from www.merriam-webster.com/dictionary/leadership.

Roosevelt, T. (1910, April 23). *Speech at the Sorbonne, Paris.* Retrieved from www.trcp.org/2011/01/18/it-is-not-the-critic-who-counts.

Heifetz, R., & Linksy, M. (2002). *Leadership on the Line: Staying Alive Through the Dangers of Leading*, Boston, MA: Harvard Business School Press.

Rost, J.C. (1993). *Leadership for the Twenty-First Century*. Westport, CT: Praeger.

Goleman, D., Boyatzis, R., & McKee, A. (2002). *Primal Leadership: Realizing the Power of Emotional Intelligence.* Boston, MA: Harvard Business School Press.

Stogdill, R. (1974). *Handbook of Leadership: A Survey of Theory and Research.* New York: The Free Press.

Bass, B. (1991). *Handbook of Leadership.* New York: The Free Press.

Dintersmith, T. (n.d.). *What School Could Be.* Retrieved from https://whatschoolcouldbe.org.

Chapter 2

McCord, P. (2017). *Powerful: Building a Culture of Freedom and Responsibility.* Silicon Guild/Missionday.

Pink, D. (2011). *Drive: The Surprising Truth About What Motivates Us.* New York: Riverhead.

McCord, ibid.

Bass, ibid.

Dougherty, J. (2013, Dec. 13). "The Best Way for New Leaders to Build Trust." *Harvard Business Review*. Retrieved from https://hbr.org/2013/12/the-best-way-for-new-leaders-to-build-trust.

Kouzes, J.M., & Posner, B.Z. (2003). *The Leadership Practices Inventory.* Retrieved from www.semanticscholar.org/paper/Leadership-practices-inventory-%3A-LPI-Kouzes-Posner/f5b0a56f4c83e0aef96094f3bb098b66b353b459.

Christiansen, C.M. (2016). *The Innovator's Dilemma: When New Technologies Cause Great Firms to Fail.* Boston, MA: Harvard Business Review Press.

Grenny, J., Patterson, K., McMillan, R., Switzler, A., & Gregory, E. (2021). *Crucial Conversations: Tools for Talking When the Stakes Are High* (3rd ed.). New York: McGraw-Hill.

Patterson, K., Grenny, J., Maxfield, D., McMillan, R., & Switzler, A. (2013). *Crucial Accountability: Tools for Resolving Violated Expectations, Broken Commitments, and Bad Behavior* (2nd ed.). New York: McGraw-Hill Education.

Chapter 3

Langston University. (2016). "Transformational Leadership" [Paper]. Retrieved from www.langston.edu/sites/default/files/basic-content-files/TransformationalLeadership.pdf.

Talib, N.N. (2012). *Antifragile: Things That Gain from Disorder.* New York: Random House.

Chapter 4

Whitmore, P.G., & Fry, J.P. (1974). "Soft Skills: Definition, Behavioral Model Analysis, Training Procedures" [Professional Paper]. Retrieved from https://eric.ed.gov/?id=ED158043.

Mineo, D. (2014). "The Importance of Trust in Leadership." *Research Management Review*, 20(1), 1-6.

Chapter 5

PassItOn.com. (n.d.). Maya Angelou quote. Retrieved from https://www.passiton.com/inspirational-quotes/7525-do-the-best-you-can-until-you-know-better-then.

Frankl, V.E. (2006). *Man's Search for Meaning*. Boston: Beacon.

Chapter 6

MacLeod, D. (2021). *Scaling Conversations: How Leaders Access the Full Potential of People*. Hoboken, NJ: John Wiley & Sons.

Housel, M. (2020). *The Psychology of Money: Timeless Lessons on Wealth, Greed, and Happiness*. Petersfield, Hampshire, Great Britain: Harriman House.

Tolstoy, L. (1998). *War and Peace*. Oxford, Great Britain: Oxford University Press.

Chapter 7

Simon, H.A. (1982). book *Models of Bounded Rationality* (Vol. 1). Cambridge, MA: MIT Press.

Woodward, J.R. (2012). *Creating a Missional Culture: Equipping the Church for the Sake of the World.* Downers Grove, IL: IVP Books/InterVarsity.

Collins, J. (2001). *Good to Great: Why Some Companies Make the Leap and Others Don't.* New York: HarperBusiness/HarperCollins.

Friedman, E. (2017). *A Failure of Nerve: Leadership in the Age of the Quick Fix* (Rev. ed). New York: Church.

Chapter 8

Senge, P.M. (2006). *The Fifth Discipline: The Art and Practice of the Learning Organization.* New York: Doubleday.

Chapter 9

Heifetz & Linksy, ibid.

Talib, ibid.

ACKNOWLEDGMENTS

Thank you to the great leaders I have known over the past 20 years who have been willing to engage in countless endless conversations about the language of leadership. The insights you've provided along the way are invaluable. Thanks also to those who encouraged me to reduce these conversations and presentations into writing. Finally, thank you to my wife, Sarah. The world has been full of people who are willing to step up as advocates, but I only have one true confidant. Words will never convey what this means to me.

—DR. QUINTIN SHEPHERD

Thank you to all of the inspirational leaders I've had the pleasure of meeting for this book—and to one in particular, Dr. Linda Stork, who has quite literally changed the trajectory of our family's life. Thank you to Doug Roberts and Sara Croll at the Institute for Education Innovation for connecting me with Quintin, and to many other incredible school district and company leaders whom I've met throughout this journey. And most importantly, thank you to my husband, John, and my family, who listen to me drone on about crazy dreams and new ideas while remaining supportive and realistic about the plans. I'm truly grateful to all of you.

—SARAH WILLIAMSON

Made in the USA
Monee, IL
24 March 2022